Contents

Introduction	4
The Romance	7
Mulholland Farm	45
The Last Dance	77
Sean in Vietnam	97
Epilogue	158

Introduction

With the debut of Errol Flynn's first American film in 1935, my father suddenly found himself an international film star. CAPTAIN BLOOD was also notable for establishing my father as the world's pre-eminent "swashbuckler," a kind of ultimate cinema hero whose combination of charm, daring and male beauty many film lovers believe has never been equaled, even to this day.

Also contributing to my father's enormous popularity as, in the words of fellow actor Stewart Granger, "the greatest star the film industry has ever produced," was the fact that he convinced audiences that he took as much pleasure in his onscreen adventures as in his wildest off-screen exploits.

My father did indeed see his entire life as one unending adventure – tales of his real-life deeds in New Guinea as a young recruiter of native labor for the gold mines and as an overseer of a copra plantation are as exciting as even his more spectacular film roles.

At the same time, my father made no attempt to draw a distinction between Flynn the actor and Flynn the man for the outside world. This was much easier in those days because a respect for privacy, even for the biggest stars, was maintained; many celebrities also, like my father, owned a boat, which afforded additional privacy and rendered the media chase all but impossible.

Over the past few years, however, several books have appeared from people determined to capitalize on my father's well-publicized image as the devil-may-care adventurous playboy he portrayed in his films. Though my father certainly had his share of faults, these books topped them all with outrageous claims of scandalous, illegal and even unpatriotic behavior.

Soon after the initial media furor over these accusations began, others stepped forward to dispute these tabloid-type charges and, though they have all since been disproved or dismissed, a certain cloud over my father's reputation remains.

This is most apparent in how the film industry has treated the legacy of Errol Flynn.

Like most large organizations, the Motion Picture Academy can quietly distance itself from controversial people or issues. To that organizational state of mind I've always attributed the fact that my father's major contribution to American filmmaking has never received the recognition accorded that of many of his peers.

Yet the issue goes beyond the acknowledgement that awards provide. Several years ago a documentary was compiled honoring "100 Years of Film" and broadcast on the annual Academy Awards telecast, seen each year by more viewers around the world than any other single program. I was surprised, to put it mildly, to note that this compilation contained not a single image of or even reference to my father.

The Baron of Mulholland

A Daughter Remembers

Errol Flynn [signature]

A Photo Memoir by Rory Flynn
Co-edited with William R. Bremer

Copyright © 2006 by Rory Flynn. 31948-FLYN
Library of Congress Number: 2006902786
ISBN 10:   Softcover   1-4257-1250-9
            Hardcover   1-4257-1251-7
ISBN 13:   Softcover   978-1-4257-1250-1
            Hardcover   978-1-4257-1251-8

All rights reserved. No part of this book may be reproduced or transmitted in any form or by any means, electronic or mechanical, including photocopying, recording, or by any information storage and retrieval system, without permission in writing from the copyright owner.

This book was printed in the United States of America.

To order additional copies of this book, contact:
Xlibris Corporation
1-888-795-4274
www.Xlibris.com
Orders@Xlibris.com

I decided then to pore through shelves of personal memorabilia in order to share, for the first time, my side of the story. I also decided that the tale of our day-to-day lives was best revealed through the many private photographs that remain of that time — most of which were taken by my maternal grandmother — accompanied by the memories that these images stir in my own mind.

I would not attempt a lengthy book to explain the many different facets of my father's rather extraordinary life — that task has already been done by others, numerous times. Besides, I was only twelve years old on the day my father passed away.

I can, however, share a bit of my personal relationship with the man that I knew as a very caring and devoted father, a loving husband and a generous and imaginative provider for his family.

In the sometimes arduous process of combing through personal photographs, letters, postcards, souvenirs and other memorabilia, I was pleased to rediscover many artifacts that I had not seen for some time, including my father's humorous "White Mouse Coursing" racing programs, documentation of his efforts to secure humane treatment for the animals who labored in his films long before the "animal rights" movement was established in Hollywood, and his active support of U.S. troops fighting World War II after being disqualified himself for service due to health issues.

I therefore offer this book to those with an interest in the golden days of early Hollywood and, in particular, to those many long-time fans of my father who have communicated their admiration of him to me over the years, as well as to his many enthusiastic younger fans who tell me of their excitement at discovering his work long after his passing. I appreciate your continuing support.

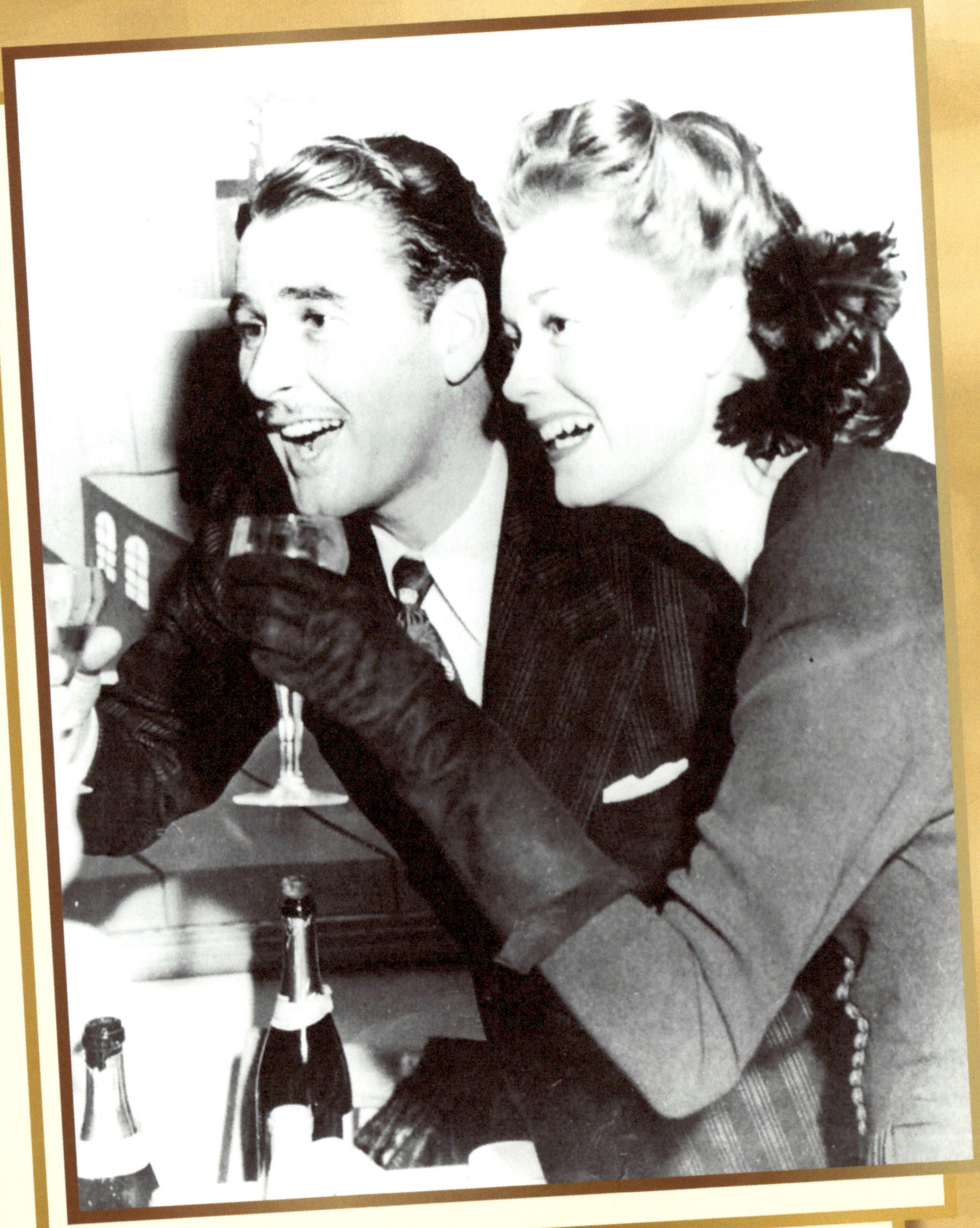

The Romance

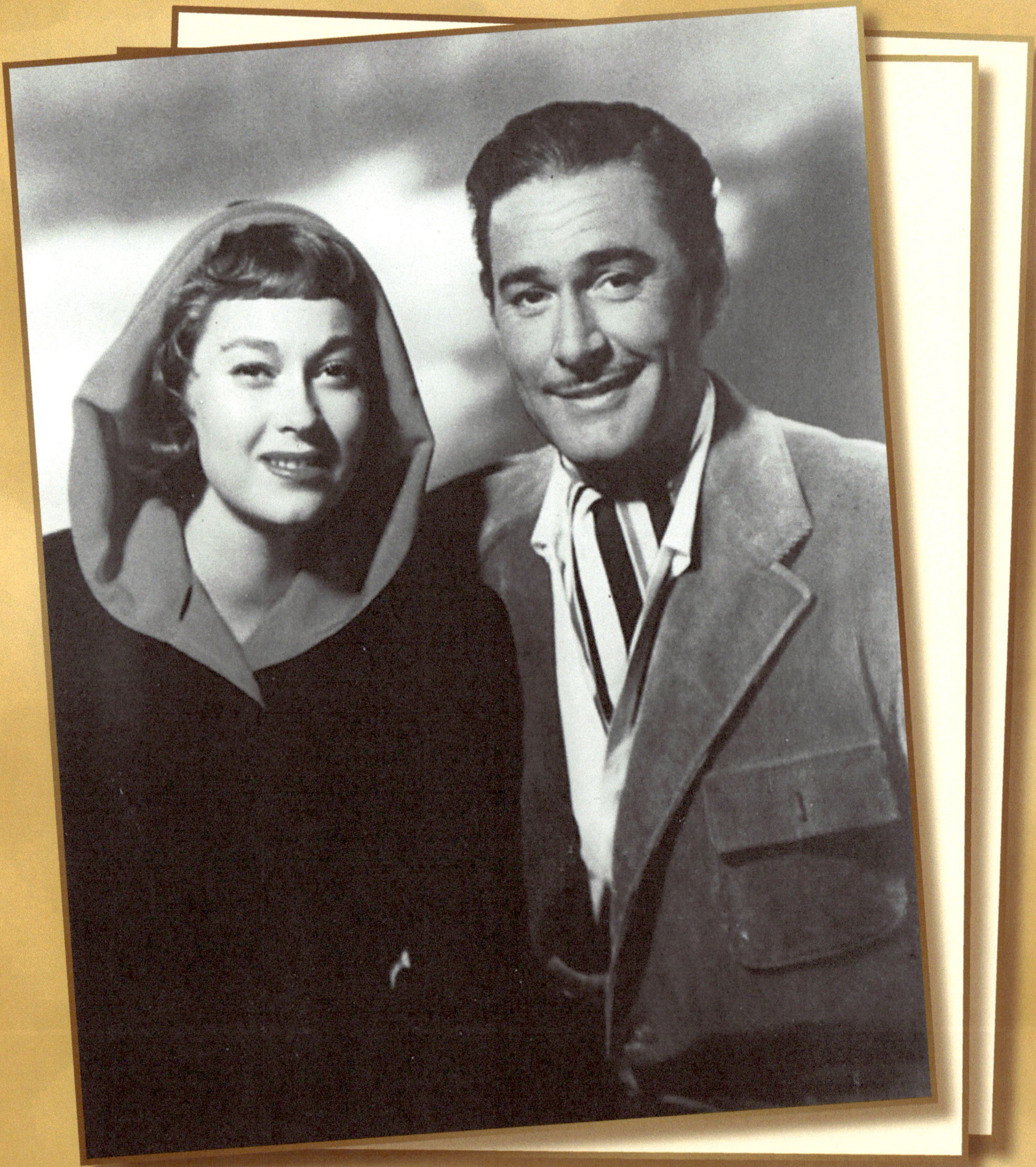

Oct VI

Will most certainly this night has taught much! Just think! Imagine — upon the mere sound of your voice, a certain note in it, my very existence depends.

It is as if I were once more a schoolboy. In just walking, my tread has become lighter. I breathe quicker, but Oh, so easier. I can feel my heart itself moving at a faster tempo; my lips are going dry, my very hand itself is not steady. And this is because you have said you will come to me, Nora, and tomorrow? To hell with

tomorrow! Tonight you are coming. Here, listen —

How shall I tell you,
Of this heart of mine?
This heart you know as savage, harsh,
unyielding — so unlike to thine?
How shall I tell you of the pain it's felt?
The stark terror? Your loss, its all-
bewildered cries? The fervent prayers to God He'd made
it otherwise?

Nora Eddington Flynn
9250 Coldwell Drive
W. Hollywood 46.
Los Angeles, California

Oct. 22nd
1944

Honeychile!
I can hardly believe the evidence of my eyes! Two letters from you — in two months! I am speechless! Where did you get all that ink?

Yesterday Margy brought your uncle out to location — an extremely nice guy by the way and I think he enjoyed watching us all cavort before the camera.

Picture's going quite well — we're almost on schedule so I'm as certain as it's possible to be I'll be finished before Xmas. Maybe possible to spend it with you — sure hope so, pet. Are you watching your food, teeth, weight and tits? Be careful of all these things and just don't kiss them off casually as is your habit — particularly the food. Your letter sounded happy, honey, for which I am heartily thankful and am proud of you for not getting in poor spirits — that's also mighty important too. Any museums you've seen? Or galleries, or other things of interest. Hope you dig up some funny places you can take me too when I arrive. Yes — I'm working like a dog. Don't laugh — doing the book over from beginning to end. Stubborn — that's me. I want it to be good. My love to Fred — I have his boat — shall I send it on down? Please ask him. Love you — WRITE! F.

Nova /   You are a horrible liar, a deceiver, and completely untrustworthy. Nearly 2 weeks ago you said you had written to me — A LIE!

Your _erstwhile_ friend, companion and admirer — _erstwhile_!

MULHOLLAND FARM

Wednesday.

Darling Ma — the links go with me, so do the tees & so does Egbert the Elephant! And I know that if your hopes & good wishes for me prevail — I'll be back from Nassau with a bankroll so high a giraffe wont be able to look over it without getting a crick — I shall pat the ZACA very quietly on her rump & whisper confidentially that you send her a very kind thought — And that you've not forgotten her. I dont have to say more about the gifts do I — ! they came from a heart as warm as the sun itself —

I'll take care — and be goddamned sure you do the same — ! Hear me?

Baron

13

Hello darling

Gosh I wish you were here tonight! A wind blows outside, whistling around the place in a very lonely manner — there's something very forlorn about a wind about a house — I hope you're happy, my darling; and well — as your letter sounded.

Held. I can't remember where I heard Held. I think I knew a small boy when I was a small boy and liked his name. But it's a name — and it's Irish — and it's unusual. And I think for all those reasons it's a good name for a young man to have. I like it — don't you?

Please like it — if you don't then we'll think of something else. Now if it's a dame how about Diedre? You pronounce it Deardree. And of course I wasn't serious when I uttered dire threats about what I'd do if it was a girl — it doesn't matter at all. In fact I think I might be rather nice — particularly since I remember how much you thought you'd like a dame.

Margie was supposed to talk to you tonight, and your money, I told her, was on the way — the extra dough. I'll send you more as soon as Warner's give me some. But on all accounts — if you are short, or need one thing, wire me right away.

Haven't seen Freddie but spoke to him on the phone. He was

me before tonight thing

Please, please be extra careful about yourself now — you seem to have no concern for your well-being at all and it's so important that our baby is strong & healthy, isn't it. Huh? Watch those colds! Or I'll clip you!

I can't wait to see you! And I love you — very much!!!

And don't ever feel lonely, because as your time gets shorter my heart goes out to you — closer, with more respect, and deeper feeling for you _____ Yes.

TITCHFIELD HOTEL
PORT ANTONIO
JAMAICA
B.W.I.

Honey — I've fixed up — for you — a very quiet but very special treat for tonight.

I LOVE YOU!! God, please for
there, I'm making a case for
woman, rather, against
your lawyer!

HOTEL MAJESTIC
MEXICO, D.F.

PLAZA DE LA CONSTITUCION
Y AVE. FRANCISCO I. MADERO

TELS {ERIC.18-03-53
       MEX.4-17-70
GERENTE: ANTONIO ELORRIAGA
APARTADO No. 1815

My girl — leaving 7 a.m. tomorrow morning for the water — ZACA — Acapulco — and setting sail for blue water soon as I get there; deep water that is! Blue + deep!

I just wanted you to know you have to separate from a dame to appreciate her integrity. Remember our beefs, our fights, when we're together? I wonder how I could possibly tell you how superior, how far you outrate in dignity, your sisters? Those Broads, Tomatoes, Twiddgetts, Dolls, Women, Girls, Crows, whose limited, circumscribed, fungoid minds, disgust and discourage — you shine, kid! SHINE.

Oh, well. So you're a superior, wonderful little human female — and my dame, the one I know + love and sometimes tremble with fear at the thought of being without — Always remember that Hopa —

Ni, ni, sweetheart! A kiss to you And Shyes — kiss that odd little fiddle Old Dad. thing, who came from some strange nebulous region, on the butt. Please!

ON BOARD ZACA

Dec 16th 1946

My darling:

Going thru' the Panama Canal, and the whole of last week in the San Blas Islands where we have been dodging a storm centre, has been an experience I wish you could have shared with me. What a fantastic place! A group of 16,000 Indians, living on these thousands of tiny, coconut-covered atolls in a condition that they have hardly changed since the days of Columbus. The women all wear gold rings thru' their noses, are frighteningly ugly, and both men and women hate all whites. They speak no English or Spanish and their own language reminds me of Esquimaux.

We dodged the storm and are now at sea, Lat: 8°23' South, on our way to

Cartagena, where, barring more disturbances, we should berth tomorrow at noon. I'll wire you on arrival. I sent you 7 more reels of color film, some of San Blas. Please, will you go over to Blum's house, run it, and write me what kind of stuff I'm getting? Under or over exposed or what. You should have received 15 or 16 reels in all by now.

You'd hardly know Zaca on deck. Took off that big sail locker just in front of the chart house. We now have a great dining place with a lovely teak seat. Just awhile ago I was fitting up a long table, seating easily 10 most comfortably.

Chula and Señor Soto the monkey are great, but resent the newest guest, by name Hedda, a lady parrot who only speaks (and laughs) in San Blas Indian. By the way, the babies here on San Blas; all the girls have their noses pierced when one week old with string, to permit the gold ring to be put in place later. You'd see one (I hope) in the movies I sent, and

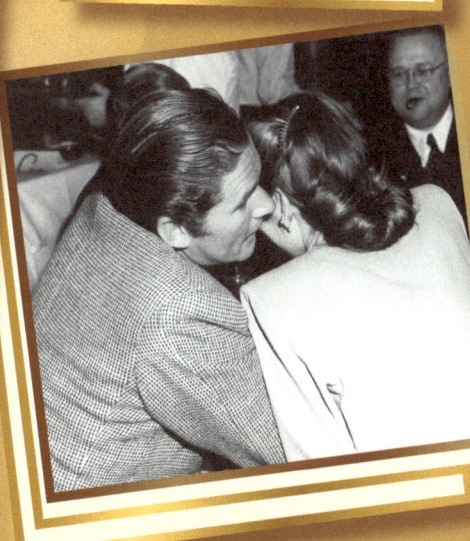

19

ON BOARD ZACA

Speaking of that, don't let anyone but Blum see them besides you and the family. And be sure you don't let them out of your possession will you.

Well sweetheart by the last pilot charts of the Atlantic I think I have missed the chance to cross this season. Dec. shows strong heads plus strong contrary currants if I were to attempt a crossing next month. Havent exactly decided what to do and where to leave the boat. After leaving Cartagena may head North to Haiti, thence to Burmuda where there are facilities to haul out and recondition next May for a summer crossing of the Atlantic, following the Great Circle route. Much safer, better sailing. Down this way

4

even the trades blow sometimes strength 4, which means anything up to 50 miles an hour. No fun.

I got your letter in Colon but was being hurried thru' the Canal (you aren't allowed to anchor but just do as the authorities tell you) and so couldn't write you until Cartagena. Very happy darling girl you're feeling well. Remember these things — this time you will have a much easier delivery, not to compare with the first. Secondly, all kidding apart, I'd just as soon a girl as a boy, especially since we both know its gender was decided many months ago and we cant do a thing about it even if we wanted to. So dont worry, you mut. Oh yes — dont forget to tell the doc you want those extra couple of stitches. one will do but two — well, thats talking. I love you — will wire from Cartagena where you should write.

All hands aft send you their very very best

me

ON BOARD ZACA

17th Nov. 1946.

Darling girl,

Just a little note before turning in to tell you I love you. We should sail in a few days now, the work being nearly complete. Pepe de la Vega can't come, leaving me in a spot for a celestial navigator; Doc Rosen & Wolf both furious with him for the last minute let down, but I personally am not so upset.

Teddy has taken over Ciro's, on top of the Casa Blanca, for Blumenthal and has moved up there, although today I guess he had a row with them because his suitcase came back aboard! What's cooking I don't know. The job sounds pretty good & he stands to make some dough in a few months work. Columbia is nearly thru—

the studio is yanking the company back, saying the film is lousy and would have looked better if shot at Catalina! I saw some of the rushes — never let me hear of Tyson being called glamorous. My God it was a disappointment. In more ways than one — I hate to be let down about a guy's talent and was hoping for good things from the Wonder Boy. He should stick to those soap operas on the air where he knows what's cooking. Personally we hit it off fine though.

I hope you're looking after yourself instead of injuncturing Old Dad to be careful. Which incidentally I have been sweetheart so don't worry about me.

How is it Hill never dropped me a line to report on the film? Will you call him & tell him he's a louse?

Sweetest - all my love and remember I'm thinking of you all the time. Bam is here & says to tell you you're as nice as could be. Goodnite

Bud

Hello my pet / Am flying along at 10,000 feet somewhere — can't say where — in the frozen north, slightly amazed that from this height one can't see Tokyo. The country is fantastic! Ice, snow, sleet, a driving rain and occasionally a wierd glimse on white mountain caps of sun. Show is a great success — thank God. All brig army + navy shots delighted, and not hesitating to tell us it's far and away the best show (including Bob Hope's) to come here. One feels good about this naturally. It's packed full of laughs and the boys seem to love it. Terribly hard though — am knocked out already thru no sleep and continual rush — hope we can finish. Must stop now — we're running into bad weather all of a sudden and can't write. Miss you and Tony and love y. that Thing, and many kisses —

End of Month.

Hello! Just thinking of you — nice things. And hoping! If it's a man, with your permission, his name will be "Held."

Okay?

Flynn

P.S. And if it's a dame you name the unmentionable beast. Okay?

MULHOLLAND FARM

The night before your birthday.

2-25-47

Nora

I am thinking of you — and coming events! I know you have found so many deficiencies in me, so many faults to bear with. Thank you. Thank you so very much —

ALASKA.
Somewhere in the Aleutian Area.
A.P.O. 980.
Dec. 13. 1943.

Hello Youngin'/
 Well, we've just cleaned up this particular place — not allowed to say where — and are off again tomorrow morning, I think by plane, one never knows until the last minute. Seems amazing to think one has only been gone three weeks — it seems like a lifetime. One can have no conception how it must feel for the poor devils who've been here 2 or 3 years — I'm continually astounded how they can endure it. Was hoping to hear from you — what happened?
 Must make this short as to find five minutes to oneself up here is as rare as snow in the Mojave. Just wanted you to know I was thinking of you with much sentiment and already dying to get back. My God — this country really makes one appreciate all those things one takes so easily for granted at home.
 Please call Buster and say we all wish he had been along on the trip — the crap games are out of this world — no one can't spend any money and it's sort of been piling up for a few years.

Much Thought!
Errol

Albergo Vesuvio
Napoli
TELEGR.: "VESUVHOTEL"

9th Dec. 1952

Dear Nora,
Astonishingly I have just learned that the girls have been living up at the Farm for the last couple of weeks. I say astonishingly not because I have the least objection but merely that common courtesy or even civility should have prompted you to acquaint me with the fact. I also understand they have not been going to school. Apparently their education, so piously put forward by you as the reason for your refusal to let them see me in Jamaica, is dependant upon your whim and convenience.

Nora, I truly hope you are not going to let your personal feelings whatever they are interfere with my right to see as much as possible of the girls. This would be a pity.

Would you please let me know if you are agreeable to their spending their next Easter vacation with me? At this time I do not know for sure where I will be but it will most probably be Italy.

This address will reach me for the next couple of weeks.

Errol

WESTERN UNION

```
This is a full-rate Telegram or Cable-
gram unless its de-
ferred character is in-
dicated by a suitable
symbol above or pre-
ceding the address.
```
A. N. WILLIAMS
PRESIDENT

LC = Deferred Cable
NLT = Cable Night Letter
Ship Radiogram

The filing time shown in the date line on telegrams and day letters is STANDARD TIME at point of origin. Time of receipt is STANDARD TIME at point of destination

SA211 INTL=NS PANAMA RP VIATRPOPICAL 28 7 624PM   1946 DEC 7 PM 5 35

URGNTE NORA FLYNN
    9250 CORDELL DRIVE WESTHOLLYWOOD46(CALIF)=.

JUST ARRIVED FROM COCOS ISLAND EVERYTHING OKAY WHY NO LETTERS YOU LOUSE BUT STILL ADORE YOU ADDRESS CARE PORT CAPTAIN BALBOA=

Telephone No. BR-2-2237

Hail the morn!   Navy Island
                                        8th March
Nora dear pal, mother of my progeny,   1951.
You who are charged with the sacred
task of ensuring the fierce Flynn
blood to Posterity. Good morning!
I am sitting in the early dawn, my
wicked little red-rimmed eyes gazing
o'er the vast ocean at the Titchfield Hotel,
where I got drunk as a fiddler's bitch
last night, seeking what sad escape
from reality I —— shit, this is my only
sheet of paper so I'll quickly to the point.
Al + Art have asked me to reassure you
about you + the Jamaican footage sold
Warners. Don't be afraid ~~nucate~~. W.B.
actually were the first to bring up the
question of "bad taste" and the necessity
for extreme care in presenting the
shorts to the public. But just in case
their idea of good taste should differ
from ours, ours will prevail. Because
under the terms of the sale (horribly small
by the way) I must narrate each one
. Natch — if I see anything I am the last

28

but doubtful about, I don't narrate. My lips, dry at this moment from my hangover, shall be sealed — unmentionable torture, the rack itself, could never force one single — — — Oops! Hold'im, Joe. But you can of course check this with Art Park and you'll see we are in no danger because of that clause. If you want to, when I see what sort of cutting job they do, you & I and Dick can give it a gander together, but in any case you can rest assured I'd never let anything by that wasn't right, and can advise you to sign the release without doubts.

Since I've just got enough room left may I tell you that this moment holds some bitter-sweet nostalgia for this always-devoted 2x.? I mean it's hard to look in any direction, at any tree or flower or some remembered fragrance in the air without a pang and a sigh, a laugh and even a tear — for the might-have-been — but wasn't.—— Aha! Well! My piercing gaze uncanny in its ability to fathom incredible distances has just noted from afar the doors of the Bar slowly opening — to horse! Love to Sam Rory & always you

Baron

Friday 7th 1946

My darling,
Well, first the Columbia crowd wound up with the boat day before yesterday, and so we have have her over on her side fixing up the damages, painting, scraping and slapping on varnish. One side will be finished today.

Welles & Wilson had dinner aboard last night to go over the bill. It was raining a little so we sat on deck under amidships awning to had a set to. Not much trouble. I had put on the bill a lot of junky items I felt would make him holler. He did. So we threw those out and he okayed the important ones.

The ones he squawked about went like this.

Chula (dog) 5 days @ $50	$250
Cat 2 " " $25	50
Monkey 1 " " $25	25

His eyes came out so far I thought he was going to have a seizure. "Christ man!" he yelled. "Didn't a trainer go with any of them? I can't go for this!"

"Orson," I said in a hurt tone. "How do you know what hardships these animals went thru to become actors? But if you want them to today lost parts for nothing, okay." I took a pencil and scratched thru the items and he deflated, signing the rest with no beef.

Oh yes, the monkey. He weighs about half a pound, & is a riot. In love with Chula, and tries to do fantastic sex things to her. She likes it. The three of

30

them playing is one of the most amazing sights.

Teddy is more in the clouds than ever. He appears all day with a towel and blanket and refuses to disclose the purpose of same. In the hot sun? I don't catch on about the blanket, do you? He very mysterious about the girl and I am not confided in any more.

All the crew is fine — but without you the old ship is not the same. You left a deep gap my darling. Chula George says wouldn't eat for a few days after you went.

I think we should get away pretty soon. We have about four more days work on the ship and apart from that the only real necessity is charts, some of which didn't arrive & have to come from Washington. And oh yes a couple of Adel parts, the same ones that have been coming for 2 months. With luck we should sail about the 12th so you have plenty of time to write me more, and sweetie please do because I love your letters.

Address in Tahiti is just Yacht ZACA care Post Master, PAPEETE, Tahiti. (I think Societé Islands — why don't you call the local post office people and inquire the best way to get letters to me there, how long etc?

Give Diedre a great big hug for me and for you un muy fuerte abrazo de mi carason — don't know how to spell it but darling I mean it?

× × × × × × Errol.

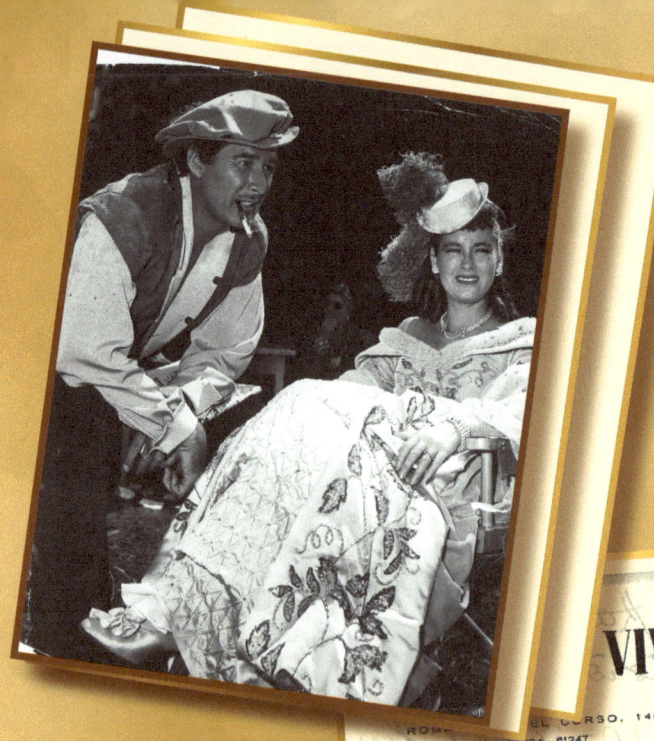

VIVA FILM e *Errol Flynn*

10th. March.

Nora my dear — your letter of the 3rd has just reached me — lent you didn't answer the very important request I made — that you would agree to the girls spending 4 or 5 months with me here — its the only way in the foreseeable future I can figure that will give the girls a chance to remember their old man, or even know they've got one. Besides they could learn a foreign language — in my own experience a very vital factor in any human's education. Obligations here prevent me coming to the U.S. for some time — I'm up to my neck casting and preparing my second of three productions in Italy, William Tell, and dont dare leave because my basic contracts with

```
                                          1201
                    WESTERN
                    UNION (13)         1946 DEC 21 1AM

   SP6   INTL=CD CARTAGENA VIA ALLAMERICA 38 DEC 20
   NLT NORA EDDINGTON FLYNN
        9250 CORDELL DRIVE WEST HOLLYWOOD (CALIF)=

   BAD TIME AT SEA TWO SAILS LOST IN STORM BUT EVERYTHING OKAY
   LEAVING AFTER TOMORROW FOR PORT AU PRINCE HAITI WRITE ME
   THERE LOVE YOU AND MISS YOU INCREDIBLY.
```

bankers and others stress that I personally be on the spot for all decisions and even every check issued must be co-signed by me. I'm spending their money lavishly but am personally responsible for every lira that goes out so I dont dare turn my back or I'd come visit the kids in the U.S.

So please Ma let me know if you'll agree to them coming over and spending more than the usual few days or weeks — since I can pay their expenses of the journey in lira I can manage it.

Blum at last informs me he is behind in his payments to you but doesn't say how much. I'm sorry — I just ain't got no dollars right now but in a couple of weeks I should touch some loot upon delivery of my present film to New York — will then catch up with you. Sorry

33

ON BOARD ZACA

Honey I just got your letter but holy smoke you really had old dad worried for a while — couldn't understand why you hadn't replied to my three last cables.

I'm certainly relieved you're both okay — what a lousy thing to have you both sick at the same time.

I'll be back soon — probably leave the 15th which will just give us time to lay the boat up and stow all gear — everything, because they are a piratical bunch of waterfront rats around here. Did you read by any chance of the raid they made on the ship? Some doing. Pedro was on watch and naturally asleep. Suddenly over the rail came six big black bastards. Pedro woke up to find one of them standing over him with an upraised iron bar, offering to crack his skull if he made an outcry. Meanwhile the others started looting the ship. They piled a whole lot of stuff (the only thing of value being a case of champagne presented to me that day by a pal) into canoes

ON BOARD ZACA

and took off. Pedro raised the alarm and we sent off the launch after them. Then Appollonio got the Higgins after them too. When the launch drew near they threw most of the stuff overboard & jumped into the water themselves! Then a dreadful thing happened! There was a most unholy scream as the speedboat propellor ran over one of them! His leg was amputated day before yesterday. In spite of everything my champagne was being sold on shore yesterday — for ¼ its value. I've therefore been seeing nothing but cops ever since and have let the whole waterfront know there are four loaded guns ready & waiting for the next gentlemen with filibuster notions.

Before I go further: Please ask Jack to give the enclosed note to Bill Tilden — what a dreadful thing! I only just heard of it & still don't know any details.

Now for my news of the month: I have bought an island off the north coast of Jamaica. Navy Island, right near Port Antonio — get a map & look it up. It's near 100 acres, perfectly, absolutely perfectly beautiful — am leaving on ZACA to take over tomorrow. It runs sheep, some cattle, and the rest is in coconuts — am taking plenty of film of it so will spare you more eulogies of its loveliness. To me it's the perfect place for Dad and that

35

ON BOARD ZACA

bitchy old mates of mine to retire. I wrote & told them about it & they are naturally thrilled. The overseers house is quaint & lovely too & there is on one end the remains of a Spanish fortification. Apollo & I went spear fishing off it's shores last week & got 4 snapper in as many minutes. It also has it's own pier & boat house and two <u>fresh water springs</u>!

Ask Blum honey please to see my car is working okay & the house is cleaned up & ready to get going. Ask him please to have a valet, butler for me lined up. Whats Alex doing? If he's fired by now, and he should be, maybe he needs a job? But just dont let him hire anyone before I see him.

Honeychild I'll be seeing you soon — am just about begining to get nervous about our next and have a whole list of possible names on hand, of <u>both</u> sexes. Goodnight me dear and an enormous hug to you & Diedre from Chula, Señor Soto (the monkey) & Lorita the parrot and <u>Old Dad</u> who loves you

MULHOLLAND FARM   7th/

Hello sugar-puss - and was I happy to get your sweet Ottawa letter! Like after I talked to you on the phone - such a glow - such a rich warm surge of feeling. You'll never believe it darling - it's very apparent to me now that you alone have the capacity to inspire and touch such depths as remain to be deeply moved in this old heart.

You know it was funny the other day - up came a brave citizen from Texas, a lawyer and doubtless richer even than Mrs John Ireland, who wanted to buy this house; and having felt for some time that perhaps a change of environ might be for the best I was seriously consulting his

The tribute dinner for Walter Winchell, at Mocambo drew many celebs, including Nora and Errol Flynn, Frank Sinatra (Louella's "date") and Leonard Lyons.

proposal? Upon the completion of the Grand Tour of the 'joint' I found myself leaning against a certain corner where there now stands a rather graceful wooden greyhound dog supporting a plant—just opposite the Heart, the very nerve centre of this establishment —the Bar. Suddenly I was not listening to this joker, altho' indeed his words were honeyed, shot full of mention of many bucks, doubtless the illicit gains garnered from other less prudent Texans. In my mind's eye, a handy little device I generally reserve for the seduction of young girls, I seemed to see sidling across the living room a slender graceful young animal dressed in black. Crabwise she slithered towards me, blue eyes downcast from nerves and girlish fear of a terrain never to be anything but fearful, and she was skinny aha her hair shone the right way and she was so beautiful yet somehow wistful that my way

MULHOLLAND FARM

heart gave the same great leap it always did when she said I'm terribly sorry to be late - - - and I growled something about, I should bloody well think so and women were the end of everything + so on and —

You know this could easily become a love letter, if it isn't already, so anyway I reckoned to the Texan as hows I allowed as how I'd just hang on awhiles to the lil old joint because I couldn't think right off where else to go live

And now for the spot news - especially the gossip - absence of which I am well aware can drive you to a nervous decline.
① Sean has a teen-age Praying Mantis, captured in Palm Springs, which he has been forced to domicile up here in a bottle, due to the unreasonable prejudice

of certain of his household 15 dogs.

② Steve Raphael's wife has been delivered of a baby, a man child who resembles no one we know, and Freddie McEvoy's wife is expecting. The latter are sailing on their hot yacht from Gibralter to Nassau.

③ Shirley Names, from whom I haven't heard in years, paid a drop-in surprise visit here, — fortunately during my absence at the studio. She met Pat. Phew! That's when shit hit the fan! She's "separated". Now what?

④ You have more people, worthwhile, who love you than you know. I mean it, Fatso!

⑤ I am a bit worried about Rory and if it could be done without offending Sam I'd like to have her come down & hang around with me for a while, to see if maybe I couldn't do something for her. Will check with you on this ma darling — we should do something about her odd little case, don't you think? Sam's okay — no problem; right?

⑥ I loved "Moulin Rouge", thanks Ma, aren't you the nice one, to think I'd like it! Thanks.

⑦ Stay off airplanes.

⑧ Are we at long last getting over our mutual shyness?

⑨ My best meant regards and a really cordial hello to your old man Richard, and after the last time

MULHOLLAND FARM

I met him and got a bit of chance to know him I can readily percieve why you, amongst others, go all out for the guy — the bastard! Disconcerting as hell, this sort of thing. You dedicate yourself to an undying hatred, even on dark nights an Olympian revenge worthy of the soul searing cries of Prometheus! (nuts, I've run out of lead. And no cracks about 'lead' — Fatso!) anyway as I was saying — that wife-stealing son-falstchin' husband of yours has such a deprecating "niceness" about him you get drawn involuntarily to the pig. He has it — especially that best kind of humour — whimsy, a sort of self-deprecating bewilderment. No pretentions, no self aggrandisement about

41

your boy. (Couldn't like him more, Ma; if it means anything Hope it does - (really.) But tell him, will you, just Warn him! NOT TO GO TOO FAR! We Flynns, vain, hot-blooded Tasmanian mountain men tho' we be, may only be wrought upon to a limit! Just let him steal one more wife of mine and God's blood — I'll — well anyway a hint, a word of caution, Richard! Beware—! I mean it! It is not for nothing, my friend, Joanne and I can almost pay Jerry Geisler's bill. Nay! SSH if you will Sir.

And to you little Nora all my devotion my dear, very dear, girl.

43

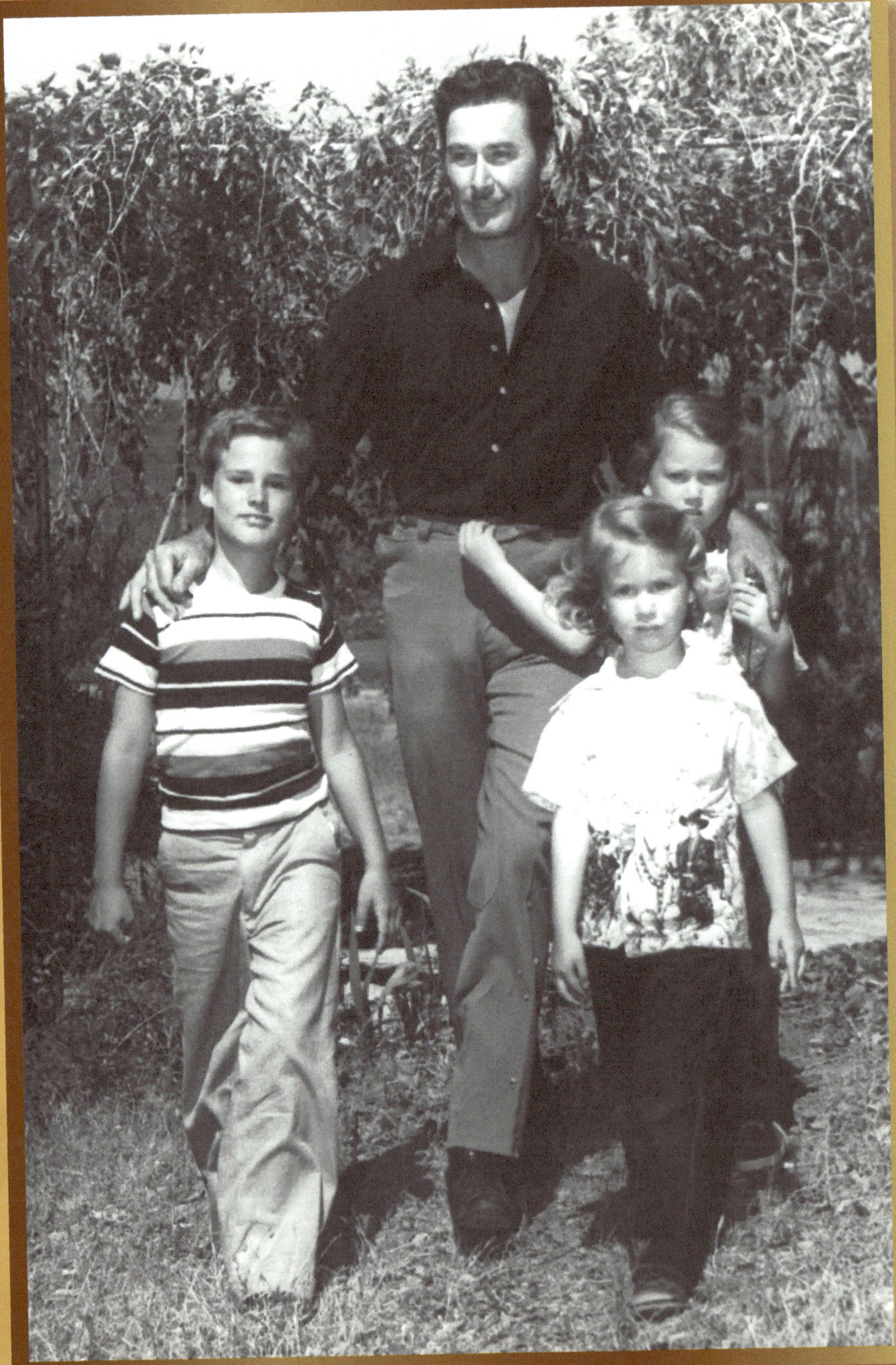

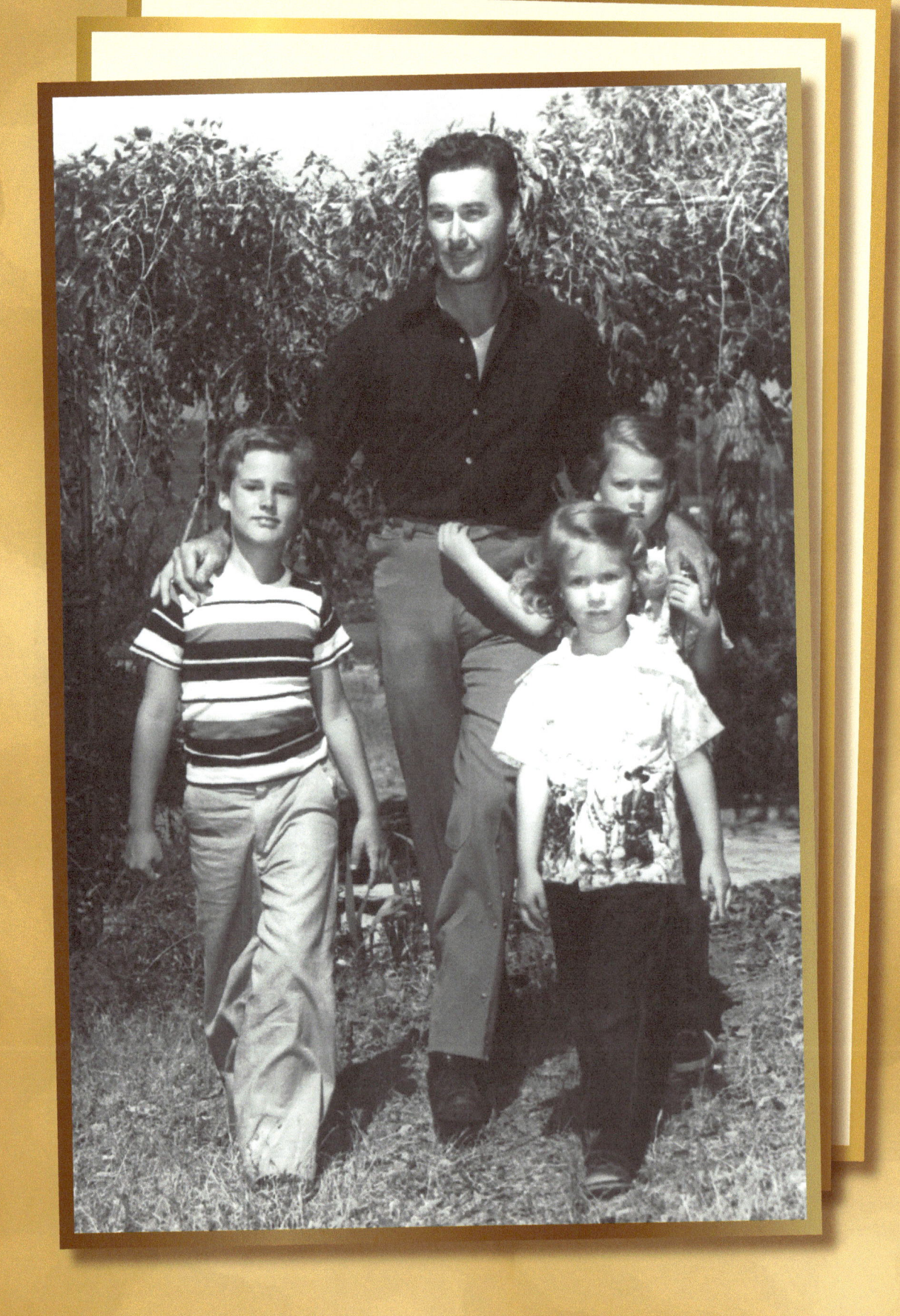

Mulholland Farm

"Late in 1934 an intrepid Irishman took ship from England to the New World armed only with a scroll which bore a legend indicating that there he was to remain until the moon should come to fullness thrice.

And when the vessel, the good ship Paris, came to anchor on the eastern most coast, he gathered together his belongings and journeyed for three days and three nights across the mountains, plains, and valleys to come at last to the territory of Hollywood by the waters of the Pacific.

Though spent and weary from his travels, he forthwith made his presence known to the minions of the brothers Warner and was ushered into the august presence of these tribal chieftains. It was their will that between the time the sun should rise and set for that period when the moon should come to fullness three times, he would labor for them. And it was also understood and clearly stated, that for each six sun rises that he labored, he should be free upon the seventh, from sun to sun, to follow his own will.

And so it came about that on the 14th day, he ventured forth over ruts and chuck holes up a winding dirt road overlooking the passway through the mountains where the mocassined (sic) feet of the Cahuenga Indians beat the first trail.

There, where the forces of Lt. Col. John C. Fremont engaged in bloody battle with those of Gen. Andres Pico, and routed them as is recorded in the articles of capitulation for the Treaty of Cahuenga, which passed the village of Los Angeles from Mexican to American rule, and where Mulholland Farm now stands, this Irishman breathed deeply of the good fresh air and looked around him.

He dug a toe into the earth and there uncovered a broken blade, a remnant of a vanquished fighter's sword.

"Steel," he said. "Material for a plow. If I had the money, I would buy this land."

And that night he searched through his belongings and brought forth an aged product of his pen, gleaned from his imaginings. And the brothers Warner read, and for it gave him money.

Thus it was that before the moon had come to fullness thrice, and as was written *he should return to whence he came, he had a scroll which said that this land in the New World was his.*

And since he could not take it with him, he stayed on.

A fence went round this property and with his bare hands he pointed to the spots where trees and flowers should go. Within the boundaries, blooded horses ranged, and game birds grew to table size.

Then roadmakers came with boiling tanks of asphalt to make the roadway safe so laundry trucks might climb the steep ascent. And they were followed by men with pipes for water and gas, and wire for electricity and telephone. Bricks and mortar and timber were made into a house.

The moon has waxed and waned until the time has grown to 15 years. The blooded horses have made way for a Shetland pony, and the game birds have been cooked and eaten. But the pioneer spirit of a man who has transformed a wilderness lives on."

— Errol Flynn

My father was always quick to invent nicknames for friends and family members alike. He also encouraged everyone in the household to address him as "Baron," a moniker given to him by his frequent director, Raoul Walsh, who had worked with him on some of his most popular performances in such films as THEY DIED WITH

THEIR BOOTS ON, DESPERATE JOURNEY, UNCERTAIN GLORY, OBJECTIVE BURMA!, SAN ANTONIO and GENTLEMAN JIM, the last of which remained my father's personal favorite among all his cinematic efforts. Walsh had given him that nickname, because my father, perched on his hilltop estate with a fondness for royal blue smoking jackets and silver cigarette holders, looked for all the world like the elegant country gentleman he envisioned himself to be.

My father was also a great admirer of the legendary John Barrymore, whom he considered the finest actor of his time. Intent on learning whatever he could about acting from his screen idol, my father often invited him to the Farm. For some reason, though, the aging Barrymore – he was 27 years older than my father – never wanted to discuss his craft, so the actor's visits to the house always ended the same way – in marathon, and, no doubt, boisterous drinking sessions.

My father loved Mulholland Farm and it was his home during the only time that he enjoyed a stable family life. He built it from the ground up in the Aussie tradition, and presided over it with a great deal of pride. Perched on eight-and-a-half acres of hilltop with spectacular views in all directions, Mulholland Farm was quite different from the typical Hollywood mansion – it was designed and run more like an Australian ranch – but what made my father smile most often was the fact that from here atop the summit of the hill, if his studio boss Jack Warner wanted to know where he was he could look up and see him at the swimming pool.

Muiholland Drive snakes its way across the top of the Hollywood Hills, running east and west from the heart of Hollywood to the beach, and the road separated the San Fernando Valley from the City of Los Angeles.

In 1942 the two-lane highway was much the same as it is today, though with much less construction and no smog. At night the view is breathtaking from this vantage point. The area was deer hunting country, but still a mere 20 minutes from the Brown Derby restaurant or the Mocambo nightclub on Sunset Blvd.

Approaching it by the driveway, the wood-framed colonial looked nothing like the playboy mansion that gossip had Dad reveling in, night and day.

At the base of the property, stables were built along with a training ring, right alongside the barn where the horses were kept. There, on many nights, cockfights — still a legal sport at the time — were staged for Dad and his closest buddies.

The environment of the Farm suited my father's devotion to athletics, as well. Besides a swimming pool, it featured a horse ring with jumps, a tennis court and long stretches of trail for riding and hiking.

The house itself had wide picture windows in every room, exposing stunning vistas of the smog-free valley. Also roaming through the landscape was a varied menagerie that included a pony and several dogs and cats, as well as rabbits, ducks, a parrot and a lamb. Most mischievous of all, however, was a pet Gibbon who had co-starred alongside my father and Greer Garson in THE FORSYTE WOMAN. That irascible monkey always took great pleasure in following us kids around and pelting us with berries at every opportunity.

The inside of the house was furnished as if by an affluent country squire, seasoned with rich, knotty pine panels and beams. Over the fireplace in a goldleaf frame was a portrait of my father painted by his friend, the artist John Decker. Numerous bookshelves were lined with books and diaries of my father's travels around the world. On two walls hung original paintings by Gauguin and Van Gogh, two of my father's most cherished possessions.

One of the outstanding fixtures of the house was the bar, heavily padded in dark leather and adorned with Spanish medallions. The bar itself was seasoned mahogany, perfectly varnished and oiled like the cabin paneling on his sailboat, the Zaca. It's been well documented that my father designed and personally supervised the construction of Mulholland Farm. I believe he originally envisioned it as a refuge from the world at large following his divorce from Lili Damita, his first wife and mother of his son Sean.

After appearing in a number of European silent films, Lili had been lured to Hollywood from her native France in the late 1920s by Sam Goldwyn. Following a few lead roles in early talkies, she'd married my father and promptly retired from the screen.

Their eventual breakup was as stormy as their marriage, and their divorce in 1942 secured for the former actress what my father's roommate at the time David Niven called, "one of the most punitive settlements ever handed down by the notoriously tough California divorce courts." In addition to their community property being divided in half, Lili was given a half-interest in all of my father's business dealings and, above that, $18,000 a year, tax free, until she remarried.

I believe that, in the end, the annual tax-free award coupled with Lili's greed and unending spite dealt an almost lethal blow to my father over time. As he once wrote, "Lili nearly destroyed me." The award and the related tax payments led to troubles with the IRS that went on for the rest of his life. Beyond that, Lili repeatedly and regularly sued him for a mountain of other expenses, almost literally till the day he died. It was only after his death – and the subsequent end of her ability to extract income from him – that she remarried, this time to the wealthy inventor of the Eskimo pie.

To me, then, it's no mystery why the Farm was originally designed as the ultimate bachelor haven – an escape from the world at large where men could swap stories and play tennis, ride horseback or lounge around the pool together during the day, then drink and play cards late into the night. As a result, the house was dominated by big, comfortable furniture and a well-stocked bar, set amid numerous cultural treasures and hunting trophies, all souvenirs of my father's extensive travels around the world.

At the same time, the Farm reflected my father's particular taste in art, too, and the more traditional trappings of maleness shared the space easily with his beloved paintings by such masters as Gauguin, Manet and Van Gogh.

Mulholland Farm also served as a haven in a world where movie star celebrity was such a new phenomenon that the rules on how to handle it hadn't yet been written. Being catapulted to international stardom the first year he arrived in Hollywood (in the title role of Captain Blood) meant for my father that every night on the town suddenly took place in the glare of the newly unblinking public eye.

Additional smash hits over the next few years – films like THE CHARGE OF THE LIGHT BRIGADE, THE ADVENTURES OF ROBIN HOOD and THE SEA HAWK – further focused public attention on his rise as the world's foremost adventure hero. The Farm enabled him to surround himself with his friends in a more secluded, more relaxed setting. Back then, of course, there was still such a thing as privacy.

His marriage to my mother Nora Eddington changed all that. They were deeply in love, as can be clearly seen in my father's documentary, THE CRUISE OF THE ZACA. The Baron was anxious to introduce his new bride to his friends. He was also determined to show my mother that the ultimate bachelor pad could survive the transformation into a wonderful family home.

I can still see my parents in the evening. After dinner my father would light a fire and pace the living room, a glass in one hand, a glowing cigarette in the other, and dictate to Nora as she would take it down in shorthand. Nora helped him as he worked on his autobiography, and proved a rapt audience as my dad would recount many of his Australian adventures.

My father's sense of humor would often insert itself at these times, too. I remember his sharing with my mom his cure for baldness.

"Bend low over a washtub filled with vodka and, as the blood rushes to your head, brush you scalp vigorously with a stiff brush," he said. 'The other benefit of this is that in the event of a heart attack, your head will land in the vodka, thereby reviving you."

In warmer months they usually boarded my father's boat, The Zaca and headed for Catalina Island. My mother told me that they loved to sleep out on the open deck. The boat would gently rock them to sleep under the stars.

During the day my father, who loved to swim in the water as much as he loved to sail on it, would scuba dive. He tried to teach my mother to swim, but she was terrified of the water, so she would ride on his back, her arms around his neck and her legs wrapped around his stomach.

'Now take a deep breath and hold it, Nora," he would say. "Pinch me when you want to come up and don't forget to open your eyes." With that he would plunge into the water to show my mother the beauty of the undersea world.

For the first few years, life was very good to them. They loved each other so much, and it was only later that the many differences between them surfaced. They tried hard for the sake of us kids, however.

My father seemed to have so much energy for us kids all the time, but my mother later told me that over time as their marriage foundered, his drinking increased, and that he also began taking drugs. It got worse each year and my mother, who had no idea how to help him — there was little information on drug abuse available in those days — didn't know what to do. I will never understand why my father didn't lean on my mother more during this time, because she loved him intensely. But that is their story. We kids were sheltered from any disputes in our wing of the house.

When World War II broke out, my father tried to enlist, but an Army physical examination uncovered a host of maladies.

51

My father told my mother that he was rejected from the draft board because of a heart murmur. This was not the whole truth. My dad kept this secret to himself. Besides it not being an image he would want circulated through the movie business, he was sensitive to the fact that many might say that he — Hollywood's greatest action hero of the day — received a deferment because of his connections. The truth was quite different, however. My dad was not well, he had contracted tuberculosis, which was almost fatal in those days, and still suffered recurring bouts of the malaria that he had gotten while working as a young man in New Guinea.

Eventually, of course, the news got out, and on June 22, 1942, J. Edgar Hoover drafted a letter in response to a newspaper article stating that Flynn was deferred by the draft board because of a heart condition.

Hoover, like many others, wondered why a seemingly healthy Flynn was not enlisted. Here is an excerpt from his letter to a special agent assigned to the Selective Service:

"Errol Flynn was deferred by his Hollywood draft board because of a heart condition. Funny that this should happen to the hero of the greatest screen battles, to the tennis champion of the movie colony, to an ex-boxer and to the greatest athlete of Hollywood. Flynn's friends say that he is burned up about the criticism and that he wants to get into the army at all costs. We'll see. Errol looks healthier to us than many men they take every day. If it's his heart that is weak, Flynn should have been buried a long time ago. It is desired that you immediately check the records of the local Selective Service Board covering the residence of Errol Flynn and review Flynn's service file. You should furnish the Bureau with the complete facts concerning Flynn's deferment within seven days."

There was clearly some antagonism toward my dad. The issue was closed, however, when agent R.B. Hood filed this report, dated July 7, 1942 (excerpt):

"The subject's Selective Service file was obtained from Mr. (CENSORED) and it reflected that on Feb.2, 1942, the subject was disqualified for military service by reason of "tuberculosis, pulmonary, chronic re-infection (adult), type in the right apex. His physical examination was signed off by Joseph P. Szukalski, Major M.C., examining physician."

Stung by the draft board's rejection, but wanting to help out in the war effort, my father volunteered to do a USO tour for the Victory Committee. Along with others, he went to Alaska to entertain the troops. He was there for seven weeks, traveling throughout the state, and when he got back, he reported to my mother. "We had no material," he told her. "At a stop in Seattle, Martha Driscoll, Harry Mendoza, Ruth Carroll, Jimmy Dodd and I all sat around a table and tried to set up a routine. We got nowhere rapidly. Finally, I said, 'These poor frozen bastards want two things — women and laughs. Women they can't get, laughs we can give them.' So we all agreed to give them laughs. 'While this is an easy subject to agree upon, it's not so easy to carry through. You can't stand up there with a copy of Joe Miller's joke book in your hand and read. I'll confess to you that Flynn, the self-contained man of poise had some tremulous feelings. You see, I hadn't faced a live audience in years.

"Our first appearance was in Anchorage," he continued. "I was pretty nervous until I thought of my old friend John Barrymore. He'd once told me, 'A few stiff belts of bourbon is the remedy. When the spirits go down, your own spirits will rise and overflow to meet any situation.'

So I took his advice, only I substituted vodka. The place was jammed. I wondered how they would take me and I hoped it would not be apart. After all, a soldier audience has lots of guns. Here I was in civilian clothes enjoying the fruits of the world and these boys were far from home in the land of the deep freeze. I knew they had all heard about my troubles and court trials of late. My opening lines were a test. If I got a favorable reaction, I was really in like Flynn.

"I opened with, 'There were thousands of people waiting to see me off at the airport — all of them lawyers.' They howled. I relaxed and all my confidence returned. Then I said, 'Very nice climate you've got here. It was getting a little hot for me in Hollywood. By the way, I brought my own legal advisor with me.'

"I gave the pseudo-lawyer a big buildup, and Harry Mendoza comes on stage and hands me a summons, which he then began to read. 'In the suit of Lana Ginsberg versus Errol Flynn—' but here I interrupted. 'But I never heard of her!' "Mendoza gives a fiendish chuckle and turns to the audience. 'He never heard of her.' He points a finger at me. 'Do you remember, Mr. Flynn, those five minutes at the airport before we left? That was Lana Ginsberg!'

53

"We were there for seven weeks doing four to five shows a day, and I enjoyed every minute of it. We flew through all kinds of weather and hit towns I'd never heard of, like Amchitka. The line that really brought the house down was when Mendoza cracked, 'Hey, Errol, what have you got that I haven't got?' 'A porthole,' I'd answer, deadpan.

One night I cornered an officer and told him I didn't understand how those boys didn't resent me, the fact that I wasn't in uniform. His answer was, 'They know you are not a draft dodger. They understand why you are not in uniform. But the most important thing is that the boys are so appreciative of your coming up here to entertain them. They have no resentment.'"

A reporter once asked my dad to describe his marriage.

"We have no formula for happiness, no recipe for bliss, no occult wisdom that we would like to pass on to the world," he replied. "We swim, we read books, we loll around in the sun and behave like normal married people. And like normal people we get bored at times. On those rare occasions, we discuss the coming atomic age with our children, who, of course, are the smartest little tykes in the world."

To my father the logical conclusion was to open his home to the film community, especially the pantheon of his fellow Warner Bros. stars, with my mother at his side. It was the one time in my father's life that he hosted such festivities, and my father never did anything small. A non-stop succession of parties began – often, several in a week. Dinner parties, dancing parties (complete with outdoor dance floor), White Mouse Coursing events (more on that later), fencing exhibitions...The list goes on...

To her credit, my mother stepped into the role of hostess very easily. She helped establish the habit of frequent parties that continued even after my sister and I came along.

Of course, during Deirdre's and my younger years, we were not allowed to take part in any of the adult events that took place. This was, after all, still at a time when children were to be "seen and not heard." No matter. When the parties spilled out onto the dance floor off the patio at night, we'd turn the lights off in our second story bedroom and open the windows. From there we gazed down on frequent guests like Gary Cooper, Tyrone Power and Jimmy Stewart and watched as they danced the night away with their wives.

My father's favorite room in the house was his den. In this age just before the onslaught of television, I remember that he spent much of his time in the evening writing at his leather-topped desk. Reflecting his lifelong love of adventure on the open sea, the room had a nautical theme. Several ship models were complemented by a ship's clock and barometer. The room also accommodated a huge couch that pulled out into a bed. Back in his single days it was his habit often to write late into the evening, then curl up to sleep on the pulled-out sofa bed.

It's still easy for me now to imagine him there, sitting at his desk with pen poised over paper, because one of my favorite things to do after dinner was to curl up on the big bear rug in front of him. I'd watch his intent gaze on the paper before him and listen to the hypnotic scratching of his fountain pen. Most comforting was the thought that when I fell asleep there, my father would carry me upstairs and tuck me into my bed.

As I noted before, the birth of my older sister Deirdre continued the transition of Mulholland Farm from bachelor retreat to family home. My maternal grandmother — "Gammie" we called her — would be dropped off at our house each weekday morning by my grandfather so that she could care for Deirdre and me, when I arrived two years later, throughout the day. Eventually she started wearing tennis shoes each day because Deirdre and I kept her running, both inside and outside, all day long.

She also began taking numerous Polaroid pictures of the daily happenings around the house. Gammie always had open arms for me, treating me as if I were her own child. She and my dad also became very good friends — he treated her like a governess. She had the run of the house, could write checks when necessary, and managed much of my and my sister's day-to-day lives. Later, Gammie continued to take care of me for the year that I lived with my father after my parents split up. She was always there for me, right up to the end of her life.

My grandfather was a captain in the sheriff's department. Because he had taken business courses in school and learned how to type 100 words per minute, he was eventually promoted to serve as assistant to Sheriff Biscailuz of the Los Angeles County Sheriff's Office and rode alongside him in holiday parades. Every morning he would drop off Gammie on his way to work, then rejoin us at the Farm for dinner before driving Gammie home that night. My grandfather had survived the Great Depression. Like many of his generation he lived in fear of another Wall Street crash, and I know in my heart that's why he and Gammie hadn't had more children. I always tried to please him, but I remember him as being very strict and very practical. Though he was so different from my father in many ways, the two men got along quite well and my grandfather even helped his son-in-law manage some of his business affairs over the years.

There are those girls who early on develop a passion for horses, and my big sister Deirdre was one of those girls. She received her first horse, a beautiful Shetland pony named Brownie, on her fourth birthday.

Over the next few years, Deirdre learned to ride and jump well enough to compete seriously in horse shows. When I got a little older, I would go riding at the same time as her each week. I admired her very much because I loved horses, too. In turn, she taught me a lot about riding — eventually I was jumping bareback right alongside her.

Whenever Deirdre competed in horse shows, the whole family would turn out to cheer her on. Most people in the audience, of course, had their eyes on my father, but that only made us cheer all the louder for my sister.

My grandparents loved to take my sister and me on road trips at different times of the year. Without my father along, we'd travel quite anonymously. During the summer we'd go to the beach or drive down to La Jolla where we'd play shuffleboard. At least once a year we'd drive to Las Vegas for four or five days.

While in Las Vegas, my grandfather would go to the racetrack, where he'd pursue one of his big pleasures in life — gambling. His experiences in the Depression never far below the surface, however, he would "pursue" gambling by carefully penciling several dollars — never more than ten or twelve — into the vacation budget before we left Los Angeles. After arriving in Las Vegas, my grandfather would leave Gammie, Deirdre and me at the motel, then head off to spend the afternoon at the racetrack. There, after much consideration, he would place several careful wagers, and when those few dollars were gone, he'd return smiling from the thrill of it all. Before he'd drive off for the afternoon, though, he'd always be sure to leave my sister and me with several quarters for the slot machines that lined the walkway to the motel swimming pool.

My father's return from Warner Bros. just before dinner each day was an important moment in our day, and my sister and I would excitedly run to meet him as his car pulled up the long driveway. He'd sweep

Deidre and Rory Flynn, daughters of Errol Flynn, sip milk while Lana leans over to welcome the duo to her daughter's birthday party.

us into his arms and carry us inside, telling us to hurry and prepare for dinner because he couldn't wait to hear about our day.

Dinner was the day's main event. No sloppy clothing or mussed hair — we were expected to look our best.

We had very long dinners with generous helpings of conversation, and each child present was encouraged to report on our day. My father presided over the event as lord of the manor, looking very dapper in his royal blue smoking jacket at the head of the table.

During summers, when Sean was staying at the Farm, he, too, would talk excitedly about his many adventures there.

Sean, the product of my father's first marriage to Lili Damita, was a "full-on" boy, and the Baron didn't mind that at all.

After their divorce, Lili moved to Palm Beach, Florida. Her career in Hollywood was over, so she concentrated her efforts on finding her next husband. She adored Sean, her only son, but, being French, she didn't consider it proper for a boy to be raised by a single mother, so she sent him away to a military boarding school. Her belief that a boy needed contact with a man neatly coincided with her own search for one.

Sean hated the boarding school and wrote his mother very emotional pleas asking that she allow him to come home. She never gave in to him, and, believing that he should continue to have contact with his father, was only too happy to send him to spend summers with us at Mulholland Farm.

57

In later years, however, Sean was very close to his mother. She sought his advice on her properties and other financial matters, and he guarded her interests until the end. When he disappeared many years later, she spent a good deal of her fortune trying to find him, and went to her grave convinced that he was still alive.

Back in the years we shared Mulholland Farm, it was clear that Sean loved the time he spent with us, not the least of which because it afforded him a break from the regimentation of the military school that he disliked so much. For his part, my father paid a lot of attention to Sean, who was five years older than Deirdre and seven years older than me, during his visits. The Baron spent time and effort teaching Sean all the "boy" things: he taught Sean to ride a horse, how to hold a gun in his hand. He even took Sean with him to work at the studio sometimes, where the costume people would dress him up as though he were another actor in the movie. I believe that Sean would've wanted to live with his father all the time if it were possible. My sister and I always loved to have Sean stay with us, because his mischievous antics kept the family's attention focused on him and allowed us to get away with more than usual. He was also called on to babysit my sister and me, and, though he complained about it from time to time, he would nevertheless do as he was asked.

Whether playing with the farm's animals or merely climbing the many trees on the grounds, Sean was a handful for anyone to keep an eye on. Because of his age, and because the three of us kids were all very energetic, Gammie gave him a certain amount of freedom.

Occasionally, he would embark on some sort of half-thought-out adventure that quickly got out of hand with hilarious results. I remember, for instance, the day he appeared dressed as a pirate. He had a hat and a wooden sword, and had made an eye patch to go with them. His scheme that day was to go sailing off to find buried treasure in some distant land. Since the pool was the only body of water at hand, Sean tied together three inflatable rafts as his pirate ship.

Every ship, however, needs a crew, so Sean began to assemble one from the various animals at hand.

A dog was first to be placed "on board," then a rabbit was the second creature on the "boat." Eventually, the monkey clamored aboard, as well.

By now there was a lively crew scampering about, but, it seemed, none of the animals were quite getting into the spirit of adventure that Sean had envisioned. Deciding that a cat would liven things up considerably, Sean grabbed one of the felines that were observing the proceedings from a small distance.

As Sean approached the pool holding the poor creature out in front of him, the cat reacted as cats will, and began to fight for his life. Suddenly, Sean was holding a noisy, spinning windmill of sharp cat's claws. The sound of the animal's screeches brought Gammie from the house as the "boat" was upturned and the animals clamored to "shore," then scampered away. Between winces as Gammie dressed his many scratches, Sean nevertheless smiled triumphantly and proclaimed the voyage a great success.

One year my father bought Sean his first BB rifle as a birthday present and set up a target behind the house for him to use. One day, though, Sean's fooling around almost had some dire consequences.

Sean was shooting his BB rifle at the target when Gammie came out to call us into the house for lunch. The BB gun went off — I've always believed it was an accident — and Gammie cried out. The BB was lodged in her arm. Sean's face turned white with fright because he knew he was in big trouble.

An ambulance was called and Gammie was packed off to the hospital. My father was called at the studio and came home right away. Sean was told to wait outside until his father came home. Sean knew he was in big trouble. I watched him through a front window as he fidgeted nervously on the front porch. After awhile, my father drove up.

"Tell me what happened."

Sean stammered that he had shot Gammie in the arm by accident.

"You didn't have the safety on. You've forgotten everything I've told you about guns."

He wanted to demonstrate to Sean — and to anyone else watching — the seriousness of the matter, so he seized Sean's BB rifle and, lifting it high over his head, brought it crashing down across his knee, breaking it in two.

59

Rory darling — I'm terribly sorry but way down here in Mexico I've just heard by phone that our plans won't come off; for you to come here and live with me & put some weight on you and you fix my breakfast & learn Spanish and all the other things we planned.

The Law of the State of California and your mother say you can't come — maybe your mother can tell you why not. I can't.

I'm terribly sorry if you're disappointed, my moppet. I am too. I had everything arranged here for you. You were going to be The "Governess" of Tyrone Power's two children — they're about 5 and 6 I think — and arriving tomorrow. You also had to take care of seeing Audrey Hepburn's miniature dog got a nice piece of fresh grass to do his business on. There were so many other jobs for you to take care of you would have to have been the Sorcerer's apprentice!!! or anyway Mother Hubbard!

I love you sweetheart and I'll be seeing you about June 1st / your Baron.

Sean burst into tears and cried for his lost BB rifle, but later, when Gammie returned with her arm in a bandage, she hugged him as soon as she saw him. "I know it was an accident. Don't worry about it."

It took a lot to get my father angry. That's one of the reasons I remember this incident so well — it was one of the few times I ever saw him truly upset.

The lesson in my father's actions for me was that one should deal with such a situation — passionately — then, once it's over, forget it and move on.

One of the reasons my father built Mulholland Farm similar to a ranch in Australia was because of his love for animals. There was a barn on the property and we had a fulltime caretaker tend to the livestock. The animal population on the farm, in fact, continued to grow over the years because my father often adopted some of the livestock after working with them in some of his films. Horses, sheep, ducks, pigs, chickens, dogs, cats — even a particularly cheeky monkey named Chico that he brought home after working with him in THAT FORSYTE WOMAN. Chico had the run of the Farm — though he had a cage, he was rarely locked inside it — and spent many days tearing up and throwing things around inside the house. Rather than get my father upset, though, his wild antics would merely inspire gales of laughter.

Errol's devotion to animals even led him to take actions on behalf of the animals used in certain films he made. When filming began on THE CHARGE OF THE LIGHT BRIGADE in 1936, for example, he objected to the use of trip wires on the horses and refused to take part unless precautions were taken to minimize any injuries to them. For this he received a letter of appreciation from the ASPCA, a newly formed association that had not yet fully examined animal rights issues within the context of filmmaking.

Celebrating our birthdays was always a big production with the Baron, often arranged with the assistance of studio set designers or costumers who set up entire carnivals or exotic bazaars for our entertainment.

If my father's work on a film coincided with a birthday, we would often get to celebrate it on the Warner Bros. lot. The costume department would dress us up to match the film and the meal break would always include a big cake and an enthusiastic chorus of "Happy Birthday" sung by cast and crew members alike.

If my father were working on some exotic location when a birthday approached, gifts representing that locale would always arrive at our door in time for the festivities. I still have one of them to this day — an exotic little children's doll from Spain.

The Baron's inherent sense of theatrical flair was always evident when it came to what he called creating "amusements" for his children. When my sister Deirdre, turned four, the Baron decided that the perfect gift for her would be a Shetland pony. He took some pains to hide the pony inside the house, then, during the party, led the pony right into the living room and presented it to my astonished sister there.

My father also went to great lengths to design memorable social occasions for adults, as well. One of the most memorable was a series of events he dubbed "White Mouse Coursing."

For these he created rather elaborate programs, which included his own account of the history of this ancient sport, though several typographical errors in one example suggests that he worked on them late into the night without subsequent editing before sending it off to the printer. The mice listed in the program were, of course, named after his friends both within and outside the film industry, and brief descriptions always contained humorous references to those in the know...

The History of White Mouse Coursing, by Errol Flynn

"The earliest known instances of White Mouse Coursing goes back to the dawn of Human History. Not generally known is the fact that early Israelites, caught in mid-desert in certain showers of Manna* every so often, pitched camp to devote an evening to Frivolity, Wassail and White Mouse Coursing, heedless of pursuing Egyptians.

Fossils of early suicides are too well established to ignore. Professor Ernestine Throstle, eminent woman archaeologist, who deep down in a mine found a fossil, herself, unearthed the pitiful remains of one such early plunger, one who had apparently sought self-destruction. Close by the skeleton was a flint knife, some cooking utensils, and the pitiful skeleton of a white mouse, the bones of which were well gnawed (no pun intended).

At this precise moment of History, and coincidentally, at the opposite corner of the world's surface, Aztecs were no strangers to White Mouse Coursing, especially the Priesthood.

DATE of Errol Flynn at a recent charity affair was his 10-year-old daughter, Rory.

Bernal Diaz, Cortez's chronicler, makes mention in his Journal of innumerable underground racecourses found beneath the Pyramids by invading Spaniards. In fact, there is much evidence that the Aztecs pyramids were built for this very purpose.

We must be cautious, however, about placing too much credence in Diaz's account. For in the very same paragraph he mentions smoking the 'Loco Weed**,' as he quaintly described it.

What a strange and wonderful sight it must have been! Those rough soldiers grouped around the underground track, the Mexican air heavy with the fumes of Marijuana, through which the mice could scarcely have been visible! Let alone breathe! (Prescott claims a possible illusion: mice, he says, "sometimes pink ones, under such circumstances.") However, there are many other historical instances, too numerous to mention here. Then again, with it Pliny, who made mention first of a certain uproar in the Roman Senate, about the year 212 BC? It appears some movement was a foot among the early Roman lobbyists to enlarge the Coliseum! The Coliseum, imagine! White Mouse Coursing become that the debate apparently waxed hot among those who, on the one hand, would have torn this fabulous edifice down to build a larger stadium, one capable of seating the entire populace if necessary. White Mice fans all.

History, to be sure, tells us that only two decades later Rome was smitten by a plague, Spyros Skouras, a mysterious disease that decimated the city (until identified by Edith Currie Wilkerson). Erroneously, medical opinion blamed White Mice Coursing. What a travesty!! The Coliseum was never enlarged; while Romans, betraying sure signs of a sickening Democracy, were throwing as many as three hundred Christians to the lions — a vulgar display of wealth, if not ostentation.

It will therefore be of interest to the future historians to mark the resurrection of an ancient and honorable sport in Hollywood, in the year 1949.

   * Anybody knowing what Manna is, please contact Johnnie Mashio Faddiman.
   ** An expression handed down to modern day.
   *** Gibbons — Fall and Decline of the Roman Empire is my Authority."

Among the many other events the Baron hosted at Mulholland Farm were film screenings for children — he and his friends in the industry would often arrange for the exchange of each other's films for home viewing parties — and fencing exhibitions for adults.

For the outdoor fencing events conducted on the lawn, the Baron himself would don fencing gear to match his own abilities against those of other experts, always with a large crowd of Hollywood's "A" list of actors, writers and directors in attendance. Through the USO my father also saw to it that local servicemen were included as guests.

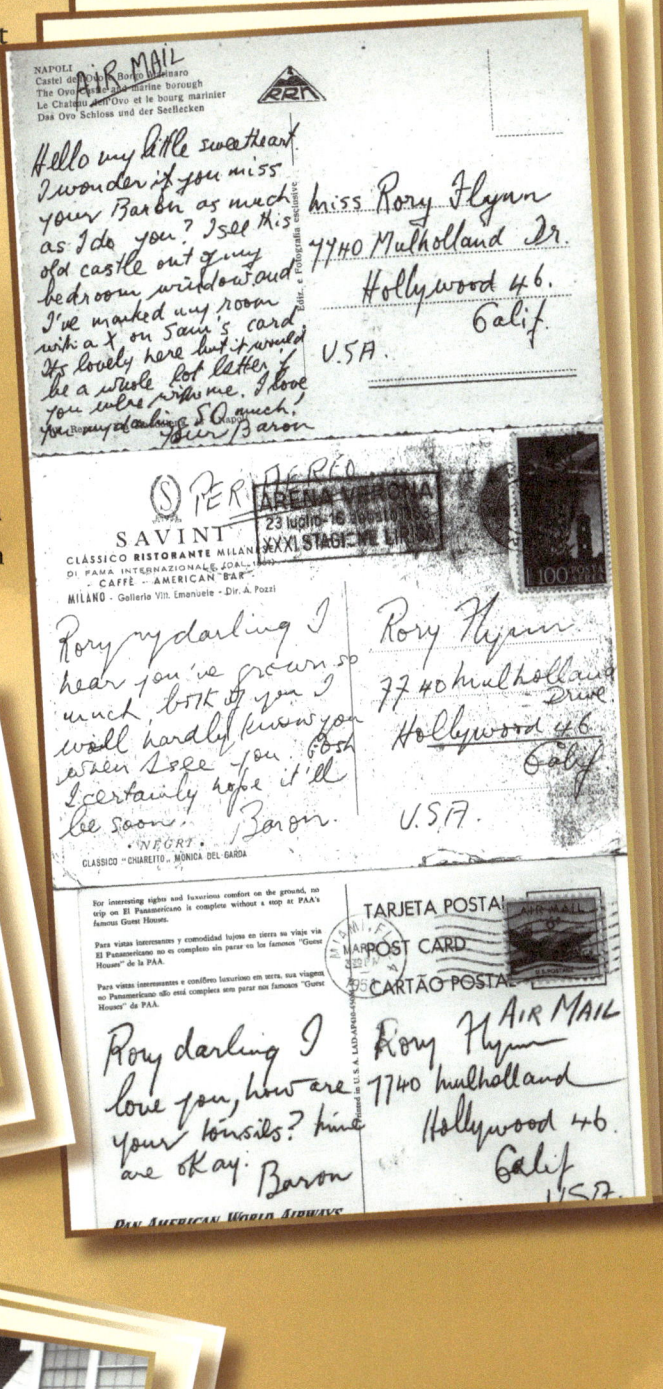

65

MULHOLLAND FARM
WINTER MEETING

OFFICIAL PROGRAMME
FEBRUARY 12, 1949

VIEW FROM MULHOLLAND FARM

ALL FINISHES CONFIRMED BY OFFICIAL PHOTO-CAMERA

66

For Evening of February 12th

The Original
SMOKEY FLYNN'S "NEVER LOSES"
THE BEST GREEN SHEET

No Price

FLYNN SPECIALS

DEL VALLE—in the First Race—Good Form.
SINATRA—in the Second Race—A Winner.
LOWLID—Watch Lowlid in the Fourth.

IMPORTANT NOTICE

THE SMOKEY FLYNN'S "Never Loses" Best Green Sheet has no connection with any other company or individual.

USE "FLYNN'S SENSE"

NOTICE--The information herein is released strictly for its news value and should not be construed as an inducement or invitation to wager on mice races.

SMOKEY FLYNN, Owner and Publisher

MULHOLLAND FARM

Winter Meeting

OFFICIAL PROGRAMME

February 12, 1949

☆ ☆

DIRECTORS AND PATRONS

DR. ALBERT EINSTEIN G. B. SHAW
HENRY LUCE "LUCKY" LUCIANO
PROFESSOR KARL HUBBS, M.D., D.S.C., O.B.E., R.S.V.P., P.S.
THE MAYO BROTHERS

☆ ☆

STEWARDS

BOB HUTTON DR. F. NOLAN
CLARK GABLE SALVADOR DALI
"KNUCKLES" WARNER

☆ ☆

PATROL JUDGES

TOM SCULLY CHARLES GROSS JR.
BEVERLY-LIONEL LIEUT. EDDINGTON
ROSEMARY-CHARLES AUNT BETTY

☆ ☆

CLERK OF SCALES

SAM RORY
CHICO PEE-WEE MARGIEDOLL
BROWNIE FUBAL WHITENECK

☆ ☆

Dr. Nolan, one of our foremost authorities on White Mice, will be in attendance to make saliva tests on any suspected mouse . . . OR guest.

DEDICATION

★

This meeting is dedicated to the White Mice Breeders Association of California. The object of the association is to bring before the public the finest blood strains, emphasising both heart and stamina, of the White Mouse. Also to encourage the sporting instincts of those devoted to such noble pursuits as White Mouse coursing, craps, and purselifting.

SELECTIONS BY SMOKEY 'NEVER LOSES' FLYNN

MICE TO WATCH

Race
    ALVANBIT: An Eastern Import. Doesn't belong in this Gang.

1st SARA T.: Someday will wake up with a Bang.

1st DEL VALLE: In to help Stable Mate

    JERRY GEE: Had no Alibis Last Trip.

2nd CROSBYTYM: Sounds like a Winner.

1st AVA GEE: Has had Plenty of Chances.—Should Repete and Repete.

4th CRAWFORD: One of the Country's Tops Winning Form.

    HOPPER: Long Time Out—Sharp—Ready for her Connection.

2nd DOCKEY BOY: No Gamble. From a Solid Stable.

1st IRIS B. Classy. Not Scared by a Big Field. If Hand Ridden, Will Go.

2nd ORREBOY: Erratic. Might be Backing up at the Pole.

2nd SINATRA: In Light, and Should Last.

1st GREER GIRL: Tab now for Best Effort.

1st CABOTSGIRL: Tough Spot for a Maiden, Eh.?

    PASQUALE D.: Forgets He's a Gelding.

2nd FLYNN'S FOLLY: Might Act Better if Gelded.

3rd FREDDIE MAC: Runs Best for a Big Purse.—Nose Always in There.

2nd CLARK G: Breaks and Cuts—Especially with Fillies.

3rd HIS HIGHNESS: By Czar Out of Ellis Isle.

3rd 1 BILLY BOY

3rd 1A JIMMY BOY: Stablemates; This Entry often noses each other out.

3rd GEORGIE GEE: From the Hurdles to the Flat. Might have made a Great Stud if He'd Cleared the Last Fence.

3rd PIDGEON II. Still Trying. Needs Slightly Softer Spot.

4th LOOEYBEE: Recently Came to Life.

    LEONORA: (Scratched)

    JACK BENNY: No Hope.

    COMPTOM: Foreign Import—Should Click.

    BIG PETER: Been Beaten Many Times.

    LITVAKA: Prefers Off Track.

    LANA GIRL: Bit Hard to Handle But not with Good Boy Up.

3rd BUDDY BOY: Wearing Greer Garson's Silks—Buddy Boy looks like Sure Breeze.

4th SAILOR LAD: An In and Outer.

4th INSOMNIA BOY: A Sleeper. Looked Good when Clocked, But has been known to go to sleep in Snatches.

    HUNCHBACK: Get on this One. Right from the Silo to Smokey!

    LITTLE CHEATER: The One to Catch!

    JANET LASS: Smart Filly. Hard to Figure.

4th TIGER LIL: Ran Out when Backed with Smart Money—Mine!

    LIMBURGER LAD: Does Not Carry My Personal Guarantee:

    CHARLES M.: A Stayer

    EDDIE G.: Likes any Track. Get Down on this One.

    Q-COR: Frequently nosed out by Younger.

2 FLOREBEL } Mare for the most Solid/of the Two-Will Beat
2A TURANTINO } This Maverick Every Out.
(Yucca Street Stable Entry)

5th MOTHER HUBBARD—In Good Form—Raring to Go.

ASK FOR MOUSE BY PROGRAM NUMBER

EIGHTH RACE

Purse: One Gilded Mouse Trap. Vetran race—for those mice who have spent at least 12 hours in the mouse trap, strictly city-bred.

P.P.	OWNER	NAME	DESCRIPTION	TRAINER	WEIGHT
1	McCuaig Ranch	JOHNNY McCUAIG	All green - no mark.	Johnny Boy	1 oz. 3 Gram
2	Virginia Manor	ALVANBIT	True Blue	Mrs. Al	1 oz. 2 Gram
3	Crooked Acres	HUNCHBACK	Faint yellow. Crook in Tail	Old Mac	1 oz.
4	Conn. Farm	LANA GIRL	Red - nice curve in tail.	Topping for Sure	1 oz. 4 Gram
5	Cheese Haven	LIMBURGER LAD	Orange - short tail.	Cheddar Boy	1 oz. 4 Gram
6	Marty Brown's Stables	LULUBELLE	White mouse - pink tail	???	1 oz.
7	Mulholland Farm	SAM	Blond—blue eyes (4 weeks old last birthday)	Mr. Flynn	1 oz.

Claims— All claims against the decision may be filed or suggestions made (with regard to its operation), at the local Sheriffs office on Tuesday, Feb. 30, 1949; between 10:00 and 10.05 A. M.

ASK FOR MOUSE BY PROGRAM NUMBER

NINTH RACE

P.P.	OWNER	NAME	DESCRIPTION	TRAINER	WEIGHT
1A	Bahama Farm	*MISS ONE POUND	All White		?

*This classy Filly has won everyone of her starts, due to her fine record she is running alone for lack of competition.

Compliments of the
THURSDAY AFTERNOON CLUB FOR
HANDICAPPED MICE

"A Skipper's Tale"

If you think sailing the Pacific is any easy matter, Mister, then you've been misinformed. It's one of the toughest bodies of water you've ever encountered, especially around Catalina. Let me tell you what happened to the trimmest little draft that ever sailed the Gold Coast – the S.S. SATTERLEE.

She was, to my way of thinking, the best little ketch on the Pacific – narrow of beam, well-rounded stern – she was built for speed as well as for endurance. Some say she was inclined to rock and roll a bit when under way, but I wouldn't know, as I was never on her. But, after all, any good sailor enjoys the motion. All I know is that she was made of the finest timber you could find, and without a doubt was the best piece of ash afloat. Ask anyone who'd been on her how she handled.

Mister, she was like a dream. She'd respond immediately to the slightest pressure on her tiller. When it came to buffing her up, she just couldn't be beat. Now you wouldn't think a little beauty like her could get into trouble, but she did.

Out cruising one day, she ran afoul of a big frigate, the S.S. FLYNN, as I recall. Before she knew it, the Flynn was bearing down on her rapidly, and without warning rammed its bowsprit right down her open porthole. With a convulsive shudder, she rolled over and settled on her bottom. Before the Flynn could withdraw, the damage was done, and her scuppers were flooded. They say the Flynn is being sued, but I don't think a thing can be done. Anyone who's been floating around as long as the S.S. SATTERLEE ought to know that when the going gets rough, it's time to secure the portholes. Besides, I think she's a bit careless. She's been rammed before, you know.

– Errol Flynn

My father learned to swim at the age of three in the chilly waters of Sandy Bay in his native Tasmania. While still a teenager he sailed off to primitive New Guinea in search of adventure and soon talked his way into a job managing a copra farm. For the rest of my father's life the open sea meant freedom and adventure, two elements he felt were as essential to life as air.

In 1946 my father saw a photo of the Zaca, a wood-hulled, two-masted yacht first launched in 1930 and owned by Templeton Crocker of the banking family. It immediately caught his attention. He also learned that Crocker had sailed the 118-foot ship on numerous research expeditions for the California Academy of Sciences during the 1930s to such places as the Galapagos Islands, western Polynesia and Melanesia Islands, and all along the west coasts of Mexico and Central America.

In 1942 the Zaca was acquired by the U.S. Navy. It was fitted with two 20mm guns and patrolled the San Francisco coast during World War II as part of a small flotilla of local craft assigned to watch for enemy submarines, as well as stand ready to rescue any downed fliers in the area.

The ship was placed out of service in 1944 and acquired by the Baron soon after he first learned of its existence. No doubt the name of the ship, the Samoan word for "peace," must have also added to its allure for my father. He spent a lot of money repainting, rerigging and remasting her, then a lot of time getting to know her on the open sea.

While my father was working in town, the Zaca provided a regular weekend getaway for my parents, their destination often Catalina or the Channel Islands. My sister and I were brought along with them on numerous times and were we a handful.

I can recall being on the boat and sitting in my grandmother's arms. Sometimes we held on tight to each other when the boat tilted in the wind, but mostly I remember smooth, steady sailing. I also remember that Deirdre and I loved to run constantly around the ship, which must have been a bit of a nightmare both for my parents and for Gammie, who wasn't able to swim.

My father was an experienced sailor and I can still picture him at the wheel, the wind filling the sails, as his beloved Zaca plowed through the water.

Just before I was born, my father suggested to his father, at the time a biology lecturer at Hobart University in Tasmania, that they sail together down the Mexican coast and then perhaps on to the Galapagos Islands, where Charles Darwin had had such success, in search of new species. For father and son it would also be a time to renew their relationship, a time when they could reminisce about the days when my father, as a young boy, tagged along on his father's research field trips.

Theodore Thomson Flynn earned his Bachelor of Science degree from the University of Sydney in 1907. Two years later, he became a lecturer in biology at the University of Tasmania, and that same year became a fellow in the Royal Society of Tasmania. As a lecturer, he quickly developed a reputation for holding his students' attention with his theatrical style of delivery.

At the same time, Professor Flynn also devoted much time to his continuing research and, in 1921, earned his doctorate from the University of Sydney. A distinguished career seemed assured and, moving to London in 1930, Professor Flynn was to become a fellow of the Linnean and Zoological Societies, and of the International Institute of Embryology, Utrecht, as well as a member of the Royal Irish Academy. In the 1940s the Baron added the professor's middle name of Thomson to his own in honor of his father's achievements.

Professor Flynn readily agreed to the Baron's offer, not only for the opportunity to expand his research, but for the chance to accomplish it with his son at his side, as they had done years before. Professor Carl Hubbs of the La Jolla headquarters of the Scripps Institute of Oceanography also signed on. My mother did, too.

Knowing the whole enterprise would at least be a great adventure —and realizing the potential importance of any scientific discoveries they might make along the way — my father convinced Warner Bros. to support his documenting the entire expedition on film. Among other things, the result, my father's original version of THE CRUISE OF THE ZACA, captures my parents' relationship in the early years of their marriage. In it, my father lifts my smiling and lovestruck mother and carries her across a rushing waterfall. It's a scene as romantic as anything he would ever do on film in his greatest romantic adventures. The first time I watched it, I realized that I would always be grateful that the intensity of their feelings for each other was recorded in this way. After all, how many children get to see their parents so in love?

After the first leg of the trip down the Mexican coast, the rough seas took their toll on my mother, who was pregnant with me at the time. She chose to leave the ship in Acapulco and returned to Los Angeles. The voyage continued on and was successful, though, in spite of my mother's having to leave, and in spite of one of the crew accidentally taking a harpoon in his foot while at sea.

While exploring a series of Mexican coastal islands, Professor Flynn found no less than five previously unknown species of tide pool fish. Three of these he named Zacy, Erroli and Nori in honor of several of the expedition's participants.

Having made some notable discoveries while sailing down the Mexican coast in fairly rough seas for some weeks, the research trip was declared a success and my father dropped off Professors Flynn and Hubbs, along with their discoveries, in Los Angeles. Instead of proceeding to the Galapagos Islands as he had originally planned, however, he decided to sail instead to the stark majesty of Cocos Island. From there he sailed through the Panama Canal and straight toward the Caribbean Islands during the height of the storm season in that part of the world.

My father knew well what the dangers were, but, I think, had always accepted danger as the price of true adventure. Sure enough, one day while heading for Cap-Haitien, the barometer began to plummet and my father found that he could not make any contact at all on the radio. The hurricane was to pummel the boat for four frightening days and nights.

When the storm finally passed and the mist of the sky suddenly cleared, my father and his soggy shipmates found themselves floating before an island he described in his autobiography as a "giant gray land which seemed to rise high into the clouds." Heading toward the only visible port, they landed and asked the name of the place. Kingston, Jamaica, they were told. During that first short stay, my father was so impressed with the beauty of the place and the friendliness of the people that he later came back and bought a large parcel of land. Drawing on his experiences in New Guinea many years before, he established a coconut/cattle farm.

To my father, Jamaica became his Paradise on Earth, and a refuge far away from the pressures of Hollywood, an island paradise that embodied all his ideas of freedom, adventure and beauty. He planned to someday retire there, and, in the meantime, returned to it often over the years.

In 1947 Orson Welles approached my father about renting the Zaca for use in the sailing sequences of his upcoming film, an offbeat murder mystery entitled THE LADY FROM SHANGHAI set in the San Francisco Bay area and starring Welles' then wife, Rita Hayworth. The film was to be set in San Francisco, Sausalito and Marin County in northern California.

The busy Welles, who is listed as co-producer and co-screenwriter, also directed as well as co-starred opposite his wife. Sailing the ship in the movie, my father received the uncredited title of "Technical Adviser: Yacht Scenes." He also appears in the background of a scene outside a Mexican cantina.

During the making of the film my father and mother both got to spend time with Orson and Rita, and, from my father's recollections, they all got along well. I think my father liked Orson well enough, but was less sure that he was indeed the "Boy Genius" the film community had once dubbed him.

74

PHOTO INDEX FOR MULHOLLAND CHAPTER

page 44   Sean, Dad, me and Deirdre at Mulholland Farm
page 47   me and Dad on Onyx
page 48   interior of Mulholland house as Dad designed it in 1944
page 49   interior of Mulholland
page 50   my birthday party at The Garden of Allah hotel
            on set of *Captain Fabian*
            on set of *Istanbul*
page 51   me at age 3
            me, Sean (baby-sitting) and Deirdre
page 52   me and Chico, the monkey
            another birthday party at Mulholland
            cocktail party at Mulholland (Janet Leigh)
page 53   Arnella, me and Deirdre at party at The Garden of Allah
            Christmas at Mulholland
page 54   me and Dad attending a Hollywood première
page 55   formal dinner at home
            on the set of 'Kim' me on Gammie's lap, Deirdre and Sean
            on the set of 'Istanbul'
page 56   Dad's sister Rosemary, Errol and his parents, Marelle and Theo
            on set of 'Montana'
            on set of television special "The Golden Shanty"
page 57   Dad on The Zaca docked in Jamaica
            My mom, Gary Cooper and his wife Rocky watching fencing exhibitions at Mulholland
            Lana Turner, me and Deirdre
page 58   our backyard at Mulholland
            snow at Mulholland Farm 1949
page 59   getting a riding lesson on Brownie
            watching horse stunts with Gammie and Dad
page 60   pool-side with Dad
            another Hollywood premiere with Dad
page 61   dinner at Mulholland with both grandfathers
page 62   my birthday
            another premiere
page 63   me and Gammie
            me and Dad out to dinner
page 64   Deirdre and me on Brownie
page 65   Dad teaching me and Deirdre the fundamentals of fencing
            fencing at Mulholland
page 66-70   program for 'White Mice Coursing' designed by Dad
page 71   Dad enjoying The Zaca
page 72   dad loving the ride
page 74   The Zaca
            Rita Hayworth and Orson Wells with Errol and Nora

75

The Last Dance

Looking back, childhood seems like a dream, a time in life when I felt free of everything, as if in a state of grace. Time was so big then, everything was about the moments, moments that took place in slow motion, moments that stretched both pleasure and pain.

Now, during the time I spend with my own son, I get glimpses of those moments, my own young feelings, that innocence, that pain. My son Sean is twelve, the same age I was in the last week I spent with my father. Often, maybe too often, I tell Sean to embrace his dreaming. It is then that I remember that final week most clearly, a week of slow motion moments that felt like a year.

Since my parents divorced when I was only five, many of the memories I have of my life with Dad revolve around events. I remember one romantic birthday party surprise Dad arranged for my mother: he filled our pool with gardenias, Mom's favorite flower, their sweet seductive scent carried by the balmy night air; a mariachi band played as Mom and Dad danced in the moonlight, the city lights twinkling below like a giant's treasure trove.

But even at the age of twelve this prefect night was already a fading memory. It was one of several memories that don't come back in a warm rush, but more so in sharp slivers like tiny pieces of a broken mirror. As an adult, I get only flashes and occasional scenes, but never the whole story.

Going back now in my mind's eye to our last evening together, watching Dad in the mirror, as he slid into his evening clothes, he looks tired and drawn. Then I look across to the young woman standing next to him and she couldn't look better. She is Beverly Aadland, the latest and last in a series of young female companions. She stands ready to relish every moment of promise this night holds as she gets ready for her party.

The bash was to be held at Villa Frascati, the West Hollywood locale of the posh Italian grill at the far west tip of the Sunset Strip. At least in pretense this was to be Beverly's "coming out" party. In actual fact, Dad was in town for three reasons: first to drum up badly needed acting work; second, to tout his forthcoming autobiography, *My Wicked, Wicked Ways*, due to be published a few months later; and, finally, to promote what was arguably the worst film ever made: *CUBAN REBEL GIRLS*, starring the same Beverly, who had just turned seventeen a month earlier.

There they stood, getting all dolled up for a grown-up party, a party that only now, in hindsight, I understand held the promise of redemption for him on so many levels. Something in me then must have known it, too, though, because all the time they stood primping in the mirror I hovered right behind him, silently cheering him on.

Because the party would run late into the night, I knew I wouldn't be able to stay for the whole event. And with Dad flying off to Vancouver in the morning to sell his beloved boat Zaca to pay off wives, debts, tax collectors and God knows who else, Deirdre and I were milking every last minute with him that we could. With a sudden flurry of excitement, he turned from doing his bowtie and explained that he and Beverly would be coming back through L.A. in a few weeks before heading off to his place in Port Antonio, Jamaica, where we would get to join them at Christmas. Even so, tonight was a big event: Mom was going. She also gave Deirdre and me permission to stay up late, and – the coolest part – we'd even get to miss school the next day!

With the excitement building up over a period of eight days, the night of the actual event loomed large. It was all so big, as if, appropriately, unspooling on a movie screen. Looking back, it seems as if at twelve years I knew too much, meaning that I was living with my beautiful thirty-three-year-old single mother who was dating heavily. For years, my sister and I had seen her through a constant stream of boyfriends and paramours. Now that Deirdre and I were somewhat self-sufficient, Mom was home even less, constantly occupied in her search for the next Mr. Right.

Meanwhile, my father had been living on his boat in Europe, 120 feet of beauty and seamanship. He was married to an actress, Patrice Wymore, who stopped working and started cooking when she met Dad. They had a daughter, my younger half-sister Arnella, and took up residence on the boat while Dad secured financing for his film *WILLIAM TELL*. As his first stab at starring, co-writing and producing, he'd put up nearly half a million dollars for the project, with Italian financiers supplying the rest. Jack Cardiff, the famed cinematographer of *BLACK NARCISSUS, THE AFRICAN QUEEN and THE RED SHOES*, was to direct.

An elaborate period village set was constructed in the rolling hills near Courmayeur, at the foot of Mont Blanc in Northern Italy, and the film began shooting. Three weeks into production Dad ran out of money. The faithful crew continued working without pay for another six weeks before the production was shut down for good, with only 32 minutes of usable footage in the can. To very few people's knowledge, as production languished he had left Pat and taken up with the young girlfriend Beverly, with whom he had already been cavorting for some time.

All this time Dad might as well have been on a distant planet. He had absolutely no idea that back home I was a burgeoning adolescent, completely consumed by my struggle to gain some modicum of self-esteem as I caught fleeting, frustrating, scary glimpses of my body as it quickly carried me into womanhood.

Somehow, though the world was keenly aware of it, I remained ignorant that for Dad, the younger they were, the better. Beverly was seventeen when I met her and only fifteen when Dad first laid eyes on her. I've since seen photos of her when she was twelve and she clearly looked twenty.

As anyone who bothered to look could see, Beverly was an old soul. It didn't help matters that her mother did the opposite of mine, exploiting her by pushing her into show biz by the age of four, then doing whatever she had to with the help of a cadre of make-up artists and hair stylists to get her looking older for the film parts she hoped to land. By the time I was to finally meet Beverly, Dad had been squiring her around the world on his films and other exploits for a good two years — all the time with her mother lurking in the background, stepping in only to accompany them when legal complications loomed.

Pat, Dad's current wife, had grown angry and humiliated. Here she was, a thirty-one-year-old woman abandoned for a fifteen-year-old. But through it all, my sister and I remained totally unaware of his current romantic and marital entanglements. Even when Mom one day told us, "Your father called to say he is stopping through here on his way to Canada and wants you both to visit with him as much as possible," she made it sound as innocuous as possible. She reminded us school was still in session and capped our surging excitement with a "We'll have to see about it all."

It was only later, just before we left to pick him up at the airport, that Mom told Deirdre and me about Beverly. This was after Dad had ultimately come clean to her: "I got one problem, Ma. Beverly is with me and you're going to have to explain the situation to the girls. I really love her — she makes me feel wonderful. Just please let them be with me as much as possible." Ironically, it was only now, seven years after their break-up, that Mom and Dad had become good enough friends to relate on this level. It was obvious to anyone who knew her that Mom still worried, cared and felt protective toward him, but now as a genuine ally rather than a jealous ex.

But all we got from Mom the day he was to arrive was that we'd better get ready and pack our bags, and that we'd "play it all by ear." She took us along to pick him up at the airport with the expectation that we'd stay a few days at a time with him, only throwing in, once en route, "I should let you know, he's got his girlfriend with him."

Our eyebrows shot up. Wow! A girlfriend! Deirdre and I gave each other that special sister look: mystery and intrigue were on the way. And, even better, Mom was now really softening — we'd get to miss a few days of school. Instead of raising suspicions of any ulterior motives from either her or Dad, we saw it as just another affirmation of what a cool mom we had, though she really wasn't a "mom" in any classic sense of the word.

We only traveled in limos when Dad was around, with whatever studio or producer happened to be courting him picking up the tab. I don't know exactly who sent the car, but as we charged towards its humming body, all jet black and glistening chrome, Mom adjusted her warning.

"I know you saw him just over a year ago, but he's changed…a lot. He's gained some weight." Pulling away from our house, our imaginations went wild. Like what, Jackie Gleason?! It had been a full year since I last laid eyes on him — eons to a twelve-year-old.

Waiting for him on the tarmac at LAX, breathing the acrid fumes of the new DC-8s that taxied by, I was flooded with memories: how when I was working in L.A. and we were a lot younger, he'd given me and Deirdre parties for our birthdays (or for any reason, really, as he was constantly trying to make up for his prolonged and unpredictable absences when he suddenly reappeared); or how, on a whim, he'd bring all my friends to the Warners or MGM lots to visit the sets, or over to Universal to see Francis the Talking Mule; he'd even screen the Bugs Bunny cartoon he co-starred in for us kids after school in our private screening room. (In *Rabbit Hood* Bugs would come strutting on screen in tights and all, leaving us doubled over with laughter as he and Dad played back and forth.)

He would also always have plenty of costumes for us to play in, and swords where he would show us fencing moves and bullfighting twirls with his red Robin Hood cape. Where we were concerned, his one goal, which he attacked with the same, albeit inconsistent, gusto with which he pursued the rest of his life, was to make us laugh. It wasn't hard to achieve. Normal parenting, no. Fun, absolutely.

I had no reason to believe it would be different this time. But as he came down the ramp waving, I was shocked. Suddenly, sadness came over me — this was Dad?...My Dad?? He looked ancient. Dark circles now engulfed his eyes, his cheeks were puffy, bloated and blotchy. Altogether not well at all. In fact, I hardly recognized him.

For him, it had been nothing short of a year from hell — his final slide off the Hollywood charts. It began with him first receiving high kudos and considerable buzz about the possibility of getting his first Oscar nomination after more than sixty motion pictures (this time for Best Supporting Actor in *The Sun Also Rises*). Not only didn't the nomination materialize, however, but after a trip to Cuba to interview Fidel Castro for the Hearst Papers, he returned to Hollywood to find himself branded a Communist, virtually blackballed, and facing the ominous threat of having his American citizenship revoked.

Compounding his awful appearance was the beauty standing next to him. I actually caught myself letting out a loud gasp as I stared at them striding toward us, side by side. She was absolutely striking. Straight, long platinum hair, bangs like those of Mary Travis of Peter, Paul & Mary fame, and dressed all in black, like a haute-couture beatnik. Her long, spidery legs were covered in black tights and a long black turtleneck sweater came down just low enough to cover her tiny rear end. She also wore short black boots that made her as tall as Dad.

Her general appearance so overwhelmed me that I couldn't wait to get a good look at her face. As they approached, however, Dad stopped, kissed her and she split off in the other direction. He came over, effusive as ever, wrapping us in bear hugs and kisses before turning to Mom and saying, "I sent her to the hotel in another car, Ma. I want to talk to you and the girls."

On the ride into town we talked and joked, catching up from our last visit, until he grew unusually serious and proceeded to tell us about the new will he had just made out, and about how he'd left the Jamaica property, including a working farm he'd envisioned he'd teach us kids to run, to Deirdre and me. "Picking coconuts, feeding cattle, a swim a day and two words to the 'boss boy'" was all it took to do the job, in his fantasy of it. While on the topic he couldn't help reminding us how his first wife, and now Pat, were sucking up all his hard-earned money. "Not you, Ma," he added with a gentle look to her, for she had remarried (for a brief three years to bandleader Dick Haymes) immediately after their divorce and never took him for alimony. He went on to tell us that he was on his way to Canada in order to sell the Zaca. He didn't breath a word about his health to us, saving that for Mom's ears alone.

The Zaca was faithful and true, always there like a dog, awaiting her master's return, always there when he needed peace and privacy. Since Dad was never far from the sea, his priorities always fell in the same order: his current companion, his boat, and his children. He couldn't wait for us to grow up so that he could introduce us to the workings of the massive schooner he'd bought from Templeton Crocker of the banking family back in 1946. The ship had been recently decommissioned following a short career as a Navy carrier patrolling San Francisco Bay during World War II, on the watch for enemy subs.

Just as he did with my half-brother Sean, when he took him to the Mediterranean for a summer one on one, teaching him to dive and sail, he wanted us girls to discover the same love and solace that the sea had given to him. Never thinking of the Zaca as competition — more like a sister, or my Dad's best friend — I have always been thankful that he'd had this bit of sanctuary. It was only because of my age that I didn't guess what desperate straits he must have been in to even consider selling the boat, let alone actually go through with it. With the proceeds he intended to buy his divorce from Pat and make an honest woman of Beverly.

For the remainder of the ride, all I could think about was Beverly. I stared down at my ugly brown oxfords and sporty white socks, frowning at the thought of her black tights, heels and youthfulness. "So you girls are going to come stay with me? I have so many things arranged. We're having a big party, for Woodsie. She just had her birthday and I want her to meet my friends. But mostly, I can't wait for you girls to meet her – I know you'll love her." Woodsie?? Deirdre and I caught each other's eyes again, as if on cue. Did we miss something? "I thought her name was Beverly," I coyly mentioned, already knowing Dad's favorite game of creating nicknames for anyone near and dear. We all had one. When I was little it was "Whodat," now it was "Slim." My sister remained "Sam."

"Oh, that's what I call her. She reminds me of a wood nymph. You will all get along just fine. After all, you're practically the same age."

Instead of flooring me, as it probably did my Mother, these words – "you're practically the same age" – clinched it. I dropped my apprehension, happily allowing it to be replaced by the excitement that had begun bubbling up when he stepped from the plane.

We drove to the Beverly Wilshire Hotel where a small amount of fanfare accompanied our lunch. As he told Mom his stories of frustration over *William Tell*, we sat rapt. Little did he know that all Deirdre and I wanted was to listen to his strong, deep voice. So rich, so elegant, so soothing, a stage voice for sure, even if Dad only did theater in his youth. We talked of our school, our grades (ugh!), Deirdre's horse, and, right before we left, I got in a few words about my ballet lessons – the ones to which no one ever had time to take me.

Daydreaming on the way home, I caught snatches of his conversation with Mom. "My God, Errol, she's only seventeen!" My mother's voice had reached a high pitch of incredulousness.

"She's mature for her age, really, Ma. She's given me a new lease on life and I'm happy – she adores me and I adore her."

Out of the corner of my eye I saw my mother's face soften and realized she was truly glad for him. "Well, just take care of yourself more. You can have the girls for two days at a time. We'll go from there, OK?"

He smiled his approval. Looking back, she must have struggled with her decision to allow him to be with us alone for even that long. She knew better than anyone of his drinking his past record with young women, and the possibility that the law could nab him at any time.

We were overjoyed when Mom finally left. We had plans to swim and stay for dinner, then, the next morning, change hotels to Dad's favorite – The Garden of Allah. The excitement of the coming week was so real that shivers ran through me...In the meantime, we couldn't wait to meet Woodsie... Woodsie?

◆ •• ◆ •• ◆

The Garden of Allah was as low-rent as we were in 1958. It was truly a perfect match. Whereas most people would have expected Dad to stay at the Beverly Hills Hotel or some equally posh place, the truth was The Garden was his favorite haunt. Standing on the eastern end of Sunset Strip at Crescent Heights, just down from the Chateau Marmont, this unassuming collection of bungalows was a place where he could relax and avoid fans, unlike the bigger hotels where they would hide in wait, autograph books in hand.

Here he was king, getting as many of their two-bedroom bungalows as he desired, giving interviews or just holding court poolside, as stoned as he cared to be. Having seen its halcyon days come and go (it would be torn down for good just one year later), The Garden's management was only too happy to have a celebrity of his caliber in their midst. With their blessing, Dad would literally take the place over, running a tab for weeks at a time. It also couldn't have hurt that along with him came an entourage that would eat and drink cocktails from their bar and restaurant for days on end.

Conversely, the rest of Hollywood was not nearly as welcoming to Dad at this stage. How many phone calls were not returned during this trip I'll never know, but I can imagine various responses once the phones were hung up: "Flynn's back in town – broke again – watch out!" Ironically, as broke as he may have been at any given point, and there were plenty of them, you'd never know it. When Dad was around, money, free meals or whatever always flowed effortlessly, no matter the cost and no matter the toll it took on him privately.

As we walked into the room with our bags, Beverly was in a big chair in front of the TV, swinging one leg over its overstuffed arm, munching away on popcorn and twirling her hair. She jumped up as soon as she saw us, all smiles. She was very tall, five feet ten like me, and that was all I could think about as she greeted us, pulling us into the room. Did she have to go through what I went through constantly, being the tallest girl in school, feeling like a freak and hunching over to cover it? Had she ever been goofy?

I couldn't imagine anything but grace and beauty from her. I was already convinced in the few minutes I'd been around her that she was just too confident to have ever had a bad thought about herself. I glanced over at Deirdre, who was going to be fifteen any day now. With only two years difference, my sister in her flats and pedal pushers was nowhere near Beverly's league.

Beverly wasted no time setting us at ease, taking my hand, smiling, "Rory, I've been so looking forward to meeting you. We are going to have such a good time," Deirdre was much more cautious and didn't warm to her immediately. I, on the other hand, was like a puppy dog. She could have led me into oncoming traffic and I wouldn't have blinked. "We've got lots of plans for you kids, not the least of which is preparing for my big birthday party at Frascati's," she beamed.

We threw our stuff into our bedroom and returned to find Dad waiting with the usual presents he brought us when he came home. There was the double-sided doll from Spain for me, and for Deirdre a pair of leather riding chaps, also from Spain. And then a beautiful small purse for me from Greece, a pair of kid riding gloves for Deirdre, and finally Swiss chocolates and an Irish cashmere scarf for Mom.

The romantic in him loved buying gifts. My mother's jewelry was an eclectic array of amazing pieces that he had put a great deal of though into choosing. I can't remember an anniversary or birthday that went by unnoticed.

The next day we planned for dinner at Dad's favorite spot, Imperial Gardens, conveniently located across the street from The Garden of Allah. When I heard that we'd head from there to P.O.P. – Pacific Ocean Park on the Santa Monica Pier – I was thrilled.

They all knew Dad at Imperial Gardens and waited on him hand and foot. As longtime regulars, we'd be ushered into a private room where we'd take off our shoes and sit on the tatami mat floor. Sadly, his swashbuckling leaps long behind him, creaky and bloated with booze, something so simple as sitting on the floor was a challenge for him. Since it hurt to watch him like this, Deirdre and I did our best not to, distracting ourselves with the paper screen doors that would slide open and closed with the arrival of each tray of food.

At the end of the meal, Dad pocketed a few ceramic

sake glasses and carafes with a wink, saying, "You'll love playing with these later." Though his drinking habits were not something I noticed, I couldn't help but think how he'd probably use the cups for shots of vodka or tequila.

It was mostly in photos that I would see him around the dinner table or at the pool, almost always with a glass in his hand. When we were kids, his behavior was consistent, never exhibiting any of the stereotypical signs of being a lifelong alcoholic. It was only later, in my teens, after struggling through my mother's severe alcoholic binges that I fully came to understand just how abused his body was when he died, and for how many decades he had been drinking heavily. (The doctor who performed the autopsy on him at age fifty said that he had the body of an eighty-year-old.)

But now, laughing and joking, we finished our meal, with me getting teased mercilessly about boys and height and posture and why didn't I have braces. "God knows I send child support. If she didn't have the money, why didn't your mother just ask me?" Dad added as he waved the waiter down for the check.

Deirdre, a budding beauty, had a face chiseled like Dad's, along with a magnificent easy smile with which she charmed everyone. Also, just like Dad, she was an accomplished equestrian, a show rider with many ribbons, and to my mother's relief, she had more interest in horses than beaus. Confident as the favorite and the oldest, she had attitude to spare. I couldn't have felt more opposite, and to this day we've pretty much remained that way.

I was shy and awkward, but I did have one real talent – swimming. I focused all my unrequited yearning for attention on my time in the water and, as a result, became a fine swimmer. I'd won some competitions, too, that year and desperately wanted to tell Dad about them. But every time the conversation came around to me, Deirdre or Dad would somehow pull the focus back to them.

When the bill finally came, Dad signed the check. It wasn't until we were out in the street waiting for the limo that I saw him doubled over in laughter. Finally, he let us in on the joke.

"I signed someone else's name!" We didn't get it. "You know, on the check. They know me so well here that they never glance at the check."
He thought it hilarious, but, as young as we were, we knew better. Getting away with any joke was a pleasure for him, yet jokes involving money, especially at this precarious financial point in his life, had special meaning – a dollar saved was just that.

Deirdre and I let it go and set our sights on the night ahead. By the time we got down to the Santa Monica Pier we were all in high spirits. I remember thinking how I had never seen Dad drive. Surely he knew how, but the studio always sent cars for him. It was only later that I realized he had to consider the law – not just drinking and driving, but, even worse, drinking and driving with minors in the car.

At the entrance to the amusement park a young attendant started talking to Dad. Dad soon turned to us, annoyed.

"Come on. We're not going in. He wants to charge us and I refuse to pay."

Though it confused me at the time, I remember growing livid at how he must have based this on some sort of screwy principle that the city somehow owed him something. Even now I can feel that sing of disappointment, the blood draining away, being left cold and angry.

As we walked back to the car, he ducked around the corner, Dick Tracy-style, and gave us a wave to follow him.

"Pssst. I've got a better idea. Follow me."

We did, sneaking around the generators and along the side of the maintenance building, hunched over just like him but on tiptoes, keeping as low to the ground as possible until we saw that we were at the back of the park, which was surrounded by a high chain-link fence. There were a few trucks around and we used them for cover, sneaking up behind Dad as he scoped out the ten-foot-high fence.

"No one is going to make me disappoint my girls. We're going over. Come on," he said, his mischievous grin charging us with any last bit of motivation we may have needed. For both Deirdre and me, this was more fun than we could ever have imagined!

We had clearly misjudged Dad's physical prowess earlier, since he was already halfway up the fence by the time we had kicked our shoes off and flung them over, thinking it was going to be a piece of cake. We were the ultimate tomboys, always trying to outdo each other, getting up the tree the fastest, her leaving me stranded on the roof by pulling the ladder away, and luring me into other life-threatening situations.

We had already started up when we noticed that Beverly was having trouble with her high-heeled boots, muttering, "Shit! I'll be damned if I'm throwing these boots anywhere!"

Next thing we knew she started to climb but immediately got her shoe stuck in the fence. It looked like she might have damaged one of her heels. A few feet higher and she was nearly hanging upside down, twisted and dangling, yet somehow she managed to lower herself back to the ground before it got too serious.

Dad told her that she had to take off her boots, that it would look bad with her on that side of the fence. She argued she'd get runs in her stockings.

"I'll buy you ten pair!" he laughed back.

Off they came, and in no time she was over.

After maneuvering over still another fence and past a maintenance man, we burst around a corner and upon the people, the lights and the rides. We were as delighted at being together as we were with our adventure in law breaking. I remember thinking, "We are a team, a family of conspirators against the world!" I've often wondered whether Dad worked it all out that way, calculating what it would take to pull it off. He didn't just want us to accept Beverly, but really like her, and from that point forward there was no doubt that we did.

The rest of the night was pure joy – I rode the roller coaster at least 10 times while Dad watched. We ate cotton candy and popcorn, drank all the soda we could. I was sure I would get sick, but we were just having too much fun. It also looked like Dad and Beverly could go on all night. I knew where she got her energy – her youth – but where did Dad get his? Just an hour earlier he seemed depleted and spent, but now he was overflowing with abundant spirit. That night the daring adventurer was back. The house of mirrors was a scream, but Beverly never looked bad, no matter how severe the distortion. Even in the fat ugly mirror, the image of a sexy young siren stared back at us. I did whatever I could to stay close to her, studying the way she did simple things, like talk or light a cigarette. She would take what seemed like forever to light it, holding it for a full five minutes before finding the lighter. The lighter would stay lit while she'd say something to someone, then, finally, she'd draw the flame toward the cigarette. Slowly, like a movie star from the '30s, she would pull the cigarette toward her lips and make contact with the flame, sucking gently on it until the tip of the cigarette glowed bright red.

She had all the time in the world, because the world, it seemed, was hers. So this is what it's like to be grown up, I thought. Independent, with no one to tell you what to do. To smoke, to wear black tights, to wear make-up, even.

◆ •• ◆ •• ◆ •

The next day, swimming in the hotel pool, Deirdre and I were locked in our usual contests – who could swim the longest distance underwater, who could do the best cannonball, the best back dive, when in walked the cutest young girl in platinum pigtails and huge blue eyes. Pleased to have an audience, especially one who seemed about Deirdre's age, I was confident we could soon win anyone over with our stellar swimming abilities.

Soon, however, we were the ones won over – and I don't know what impressed us more, the fact that she had a hotel towel in her hand (a guest!...another cohort!) or the fact that we finally recognized her as Patty McCormack, child star of The Bad Seed. In no time she and Deirdre became fast friends and started racing pool lengths together, leaving me to fend for myself.

I went back to the room to read another in my endless chain of books about animals, horses and dogs – if it had fur and four legs, it was in my hands. The front door to the bungalow was unlocked (one of Dad's policies), so I went in and found Beverly sitting on Dad's lap. They continued kissing passionately, the sounds of "Queen for a Day" hiding my intrusion, I thought. They had been down at the pool earlier, but had come back for beverages and had clearly gotten distracted. He was in swim shorts with his terrycloth robe and she had a sarong over her gold lamé two-piece bathing suit.

I instinctively spun around and started to quietly sneak back out until, "Hey, where are you going, darling?" I stopped and turned, discomfort oozing from every pore in my body.

"Comeback and sit with us. I have been meaning to tell you how much I adore Woodsie."

As they continued packing at each other, I thought it looked so bizarre: he seemed so old and she barely one-third his age. What does she see in him, I wondered, but I got my answer in my next awkward breath, as they gazed deeply into each other's eyes. As odd as it seemed, there was no denying that their connection was both intimate and real. Though I fought the emotions, I have to admit that, even then, it honestly moved me.

"You are going to grow up and look just like Woodsie," he said, looking over and smiling.

Was it a joke? Was he making fun of me? I was used to it because my sister was a merciless tease, but no, I looked again and saw that he was serious. I crept closer and he lifted up my chin. "Honest."
He examined Beverly like an anatomy professor. "See, look that these legs, long and beautiful, just like yours are already. You'll be tall like Woodsie and clothes will always look great on you. Models are tall and thin. And look at this..."

He cupped one of her petite breasts in his hand.

"Just a handful – that's what I like in a woman: small breasts and long legs."

In spite of his scientific manner I already felt myself flushing with embarrassment. To her credit, Beverly immediately sensed my discomfort and said, "Okay, enough lessons for today. Let's all go for a swim."

And we did.

It was years before I understood her being with him, Dad's words, all of it. At the moment, though, I guess my big fear was that I would never stop growing, never have breasts.

Somehow Dad knew my secret, what was bothering me the most, and found his way of dealing with it — by comparing me with Beverly and giving me the Ugly Duckling speech. It was a valiant effort to lift my non-existent self-esteem.

Beverly and I sat by the pool talking while Dad fell asleep in the warm California sun and Deirdre and Patty remained thoroughly occupied playing water polo. I couldn't help but think how different Patty and I were, though raised in the same town and just five years apart. Connected by the odd link of my father's unrelenting hunger for youth, it was then that I realized that she could end up being my stepmother.

"What do you see in him? He's so old." I'd finally worked up the courage.

Beverly smiled — there was so much I didn't know.

"He's not so old...and no one has ever treated me like this, like a queen. With a good diet and less booze he could look much younger and that is my mission, to get him in shape."
She had a big job ahead of her. He would need a good diet, lots of exercise, and no booze. God only knew if and when she'd be able to pull off this feat and get the regimen started, but I honestly felt her motives were pure.

Today, as a grown woman, I see it a little differently. Simply put, she wanted to be taught and he wanted to teach. And her story had a familiar ring to it, cut, as it were, from the same cloth as my mother's. Being underage, having to call her mother for permission to hang out with Errol. The reason why Mom was so permissive that week must have been that she looked at Beverly and saw so much of herself in the young woman. But at that moment I saw Beverly as something completely other and had so many questions I wanted to ask, I didn't know where to start. Where did she come from? How did she get here?

And the stories came rolling out of her, starting with how she had begun working when she was four years old and ending with a sentimental recounting of her first date at Imperial Gardens with Dad.

"I still have the sake jugs," she smiled, then, lifting her face back toward me, added, "We're in love and very happy."
I couldn't dispute that they were in love, especially since Dad was willing to take great and somewhat questionable risks at this very delicate juncture in his career because of his infatuation. For example, he had recently read Nabokob's Lolita and decided he wanted to play the part of professor Humbert. He called Ron Shedlow, his secretary who maintained his business relationships while Dad globe-trotted, and asked him to set up a meeting while he was visiting us.

Kubrick's reported response was, "Great. Call as soon as he gets in. We'd love to see him," which they did. Ron drove Dad to Kubrick's offices at Universal and they spent a half hour together, good humor leaking out under the door.

But as Dad came out, he turned to Ron, downcast. "I don't think it's going to happen."

Ron asked why not, since Kubrick had seemed so interested.

Dad looked at him point-blank. "He doesn't think Beverly can do it."
As it was later explained to me, Dad presented it as an ultimatum that Beverly be cast in the title role, something with Kubrick couldn't buy, no matter how much he may have wanted Dad for the part.

◆•••◆•••◆

All during this time Dad was not only busy spoiling us with his love and affection, but with anything we wanted, as well. This as our time and he only made business appointments for the few days we spent back home with Mom or at school.

One afternoon in the middle of the week we set off to watch Deirdre jump her horse. All us Flynn kids were blessed with Dad's strength and agility, and after several years of equine training she was something to see. Unfortunately, the last time she took Dad to a show jumping event, to our horror he stole the show, ending up so preoccupied with signing autographs that he never saw her win first place. Although she was inwardly crushed at the time, outwardly she made a stoic attempt to not reveal her disappointment.

On this day, not to be outdone, I kept trying to get Dad alone long enough to brag about my recent triumphs at my school's swim meets. Swimming was one of the few things I did with pure, unselfconscious passion. It was one area about which I was able to hold my head high. In addition, my hard work had been rewarded with a slew of blue ribbons, most coming from my mastering the backstroke.

But as we sat in the mostly empty stands of Burbank's Pickwick Equestrian Center, breathing the warm, dust-coated late afternoon air, my words fell on deaf ears. Determined not to repeat what happened the last time he attended one of Deirdre's events, Dad's focus was intense, and intensely on her. It seemed that while Deirdre could make contact with him from atop a beautiful seven-foot steed a couple of hundred feet away, I couldn't touch him from just the next seat.

Though this sort of focus was incredibly rare for him – his time with us was brief and always challenged by an array of distractions – Dad loved taking his girls around and introducing us like grown-ups to all his friends. He had an unwavering pride in us, his kids, and what and who we were becoming.

And we'd rarely disappoint. We saw the upcoming dig at Frascati's as another occasion to shine like we had two years earlier when he took Deirdre and me to the premiere at Grauman's Chinese Theater of *My Man Godfrey* starring Dad's buddy David Niven. It was our first exposure to the full treatment: red carpet, Kleig lights, screaming fans and all. As we stepped out of the limo and flashbulbs began popping, Deirdre and I each took one of Dad's arms. The crowd screamed, "Look here, Errol!! Over here!!" He had told us not to rush, but to walk slow while he said hello and waved, smiling his bright trademark smile.
It was then that I realized what a star was, what it meant to be loved and adored. At that moment, Dad was the biggest man in the world to me. I hadn't really understood it fully until then, since we had only heard about his "stardom," never seeing this sort of scene before. Here in front of us was another unarguable side of his life – the public showing how they felt – his interplay with them, the lights, the press, the whole machine. I remember suddenly getting a shiver as I realized he wasn't just to be shared amongst his women, but the entire planet. But that had been two years ago.

It was different now. Much different.

The morning after Deirdre's horse show, I woke up at The Garden of Allah feeling terrible. It was my grandmother whom I cried for when I got sick. (Since my Mom was usually off managing the clothing boutique in Beverly Hills she worked at to make ends meet, she would invariably call her mother in to help care for us at times like this.) But Dad was here now, and without hesitation he stepped right in. He got a cool washcloth for my forehead, then called the manager for a thermometer.

Yes, it turned out I had a slight fever, and when my stomach started to hurt Dad decided he'd better call the doctor. He had me lie down on the couch, then he piled blankets on top of me. As he dug through his phone book for the doctor's number, he kept taking the thermometer in and out of my mouth, too flustered to leave it in long enough to get an accurate reading.

I had to restrain myself from laughing as he frowned down at me with that scrunched up look on his face, like he was puzzling over some cryptic markings etched in my forehead. Still, he continued walking around, asking me over and over how I felt, and whether anything had changed. No, I still felt like crap.

He called Beverly over — "Feel her forehead. Do you think she has a temperature?"

Beverly leaned over me and put her hand on my forehead. After about three minutes of agonizing suspense, she shrugged and mumbled, "I dunno" through a big wad of gum she cracked between her teeth before heading back to the bedroom.

By now I had started to sweat from all the blankets on me, but Dad kept at it with the thermometer, only giving up when Dr. Nolan with his little black bag finally knocked at the door. I swung from humor to fear, since I knew from past experience that the good doctor was capable of giving outrageously painful shots. He, too, frowned down at me with that perplexed look, felt around, then finally brought out some pills. I was pronounced underweight and diagnosed with "allergies." Along with the pills, he left some syrup behind for me to take once every four hours.

I soon started feeling better, perhaps just because the drama was over. But I'll never forget the concern and guilt written across Dad's face as I lay there — as if the incident had brought back afresh the fact he'd missed a particularly painful surgery of mine four years earlier. He had been off shooting a film in Europe while I suffered through an emergency appendectomy, and while I had long since forgiven his absence, it was clear he hadn't.

When I awoke the next morning feeling myself again, Dad was already dressed and looking dapper. He announced he wanted to see some old sites and while we got dressed, he called for the car. He loved seafood and for lunch we hit Roy's, a small favorite spot of his at the western edge of Santa Monica Canyon, along the Pacific Coast Highway. We ate a big meal that he hooted over, shaking the hand of the chef, tipping the waiter heavily, then likely signing someone else's name on the check.

Afterwards, we headed north along the coast for about an hour, to the Ventura County line, to a little beach with a private cove that only local surfers knew about. We sat on the beach, watching the fishermen baiting and casting their lines. Deirdre and Beverly went for a walk. As Dad and I sat alone, I again attempted to tell him about my swimming. Suddenly, I heard Beverly and Deirdre screaming for us.

We jumped up and rand down the shore to where Beverly was shouting, "Errol, look, he's hurt! We've gotta help!" She pointed out towards a dorsal fin going round and round in circles as she pushed Dad towards the water. Thinking it was a shark, I shot back up the sand until Beverly turned back and called, "Rory, go knock on that neighbor's door. Ask them to call the Sealife Rescue. Hurry, he's dying!"

Dad, already in the water, began swimming calmly out towards the fin. I, on the other hand, was convinced he was about to be ripped from limb to limb, and the expression on my face, I was later told, was something out of a B horror film. I turned and ran, but kept looking back until I finally saw Dad standing waist deep in the water, gently cradling a badly wounded dolphin, helping it to swim as it if were his own child.

The rescuers finally came and the dolphin was taken away. We never found out if it survived. It had been sliced by the propeller of a fishing boat and the cut had been deep. The strongest memory that remains from that day, however, is the intense sense of pride Deirdre, Beverly and I felt. In our eyes, my Dad was simply the best.

◆◆◆◆◆

As the night of the actual party grew closer, there was much ceremony, not least of which included going out shopping with Beverly for a dress. After stopping at virtually every boutique in Beverly Hills, she ended up with two sleek cocktail numbers — both black, to no one's surprise. Since Mom had already picked out what Deirdre and I were to wear, and there'd be no changing that, Dad kept himself busy during these outings, mercilessly teasing us and plying Beverly with compliments that would make her shine even brighter as she tried on one outfit after the next.

Late on the afternoon of the party, Beverly invited me to help her choose what she'd actually wear that night. I sat on the bed, legs crossed, while she put on a virtual fashion show, one outfit after the other. Since her entire wardrobe was black, she ended up trying on at least a half dozen dresses, all of them nearly identical, asking my detailed opinion on why I like this one over that one — something I always loved doing with Mom.

Though she only took a few bits of my advice here and there, I was too giddy with the fun of it all to be offended. In the end she wound up with the simplest of them all: a tight, spaghetti-strap, knee-length cocktail dress, to which she added long black satin gloves that elevated her appearance to a completely other level. Since Dad wasn't much for makeup, a smudge of lipstick and mascara and she was ready. Though it was a relatively simple transformation, it seemed to take hours and left her looking adorable, sexy and classy.

Conversely, I just tumbled right into my clothes: a beautiful white gingham dress with navy polka dots with a big petticoat underneath that I flounced out just enough to feel dressy. Under strict orders from Mom, I was to wear my hair in a ponytail, along with flats and socks, all of which I was convinced just added to my goofball factor. Deirdre, on the other hand, wore a tweed suit with dark heels, her hair done up Lauren Bacall-style.

Frascati's filled up fast and it seemed everyone who was anyone was indeed there. It was only later I found out who wrong I was. Yes, it was crowded, but the closer I looked, the more I realized they were almost all unfamiliar faces — mostly Beverly's friends. I knew Dad was expecting a lot more of his old pals to show.

Where was Gary Cooper, our good friend who had come up every weekend to Mulholland to play tennis, or Dad's co-star Alexis Smith, who also lived in town and was a regular at our house?

Micky Rooney was there, always a true friend til the end. I couldn't help but remember back to those parties at Mulholland – the gardenias, the mariachis, the wild games, the times where everyone wanted to be my father's friend. Though I didn't know to what degree, even to me, a clare sense of abandonment hung in the air.

Dad's virile good looks were little more than a memory at this point – his slim athletic waistline had long since sagged into a visible bulge – but he still walked tall and proud and charmed everyone he met, male and female. His eyes, though still the same rich hazel, were now bloodshot and buried deep in dark, swollen sockets. His nose, once so beautifully carved, could now have easily been mistaken for that of W. C. Fields.

Dad rose to say a little something to his assembled guests. He pulled me, Deirdre and Beverly to the entrance of the restaurant and told everyone that this was indeed a special occasion, thanking them for coming and hoping they would enjoy their meal. He then introduced Beverly as the star of his new film – and as the star of his life. He told them how very talented she was, than made a joke about her being underage.

Right around then, I just remember trying to melt, to face away completely. I started back up slowly, needing to hide from sight my flushed, embarrassed face, which glowed like neon. But right then, Dad's arm reached back and pulled me in front of him as he introduced Deirdre and me to the room. "His family" were the words he used as he went on. Though the embarrassment eased, being replaced by a slight feeling of security due to his standing right beside me, all I could do was smile and give an awkward wave.

He then grew serious and talked a bit about how he'd been living and writing his autobiography all these years. Now the book was finally finished and would be published in December, two months from then. He smiled and added that the public might enjoy the truth about him for a change. Finally, he toasted the crowd, giving me a chance to peel away and try to blend back into the scenery.

Though food was the last thing on our minds, Deirdre and I downed plates of hors d'oeuvres and spaghetti while schmoozing with those who came to see us, taking our cue from Dad's jovial performance. It was as if we were the receiving line for a wedding or bar mitzvah — meeting one gin-soaked face after the next, people I had never seen before, nor would see again.

As the night wore on, the crowd seemed to grow friendlier and sloppier, downing one round of free booze after another. Their questions became rote, as did our answers: yes, we have grown (especially me); yes, I'm doing just fine in school (a horrible lie); yes, everything is just wonderful at home (one more lie can't hurt); yes, my mother also is doing great; and most importantly, yes, we are all one big happy family.

I glanced over to Mom. She was absolutely shining. Her beauty was at its peak and she knew it, allowing her to effortlessly command any room she entered. In her prime at thirty-three, she was still dating with a vengeance, continuing on in her shameless hunt for her next husband. She had about ten boyfriends, most of whom made advances to me that I constantly fended off, and whom I now see as part of a constant procession of prospective pedophiles — all with too keen an interest in the underdeveloped physique of a twelve-year-old.

Whereas Beverly may have had youth on her side, Mom had gusto and was ripe for the occasion. Fifteen years earlier she may have been the coquettish and flirty young lade Beverly was now, but currently she was in full command of her self and her femininity, creating an irresistible package for the likes of Peter Lawford, Scott Brady, Jimmy Van Heusen and Frank Sinatra, all of whom she had dated without concern for the others finding out.

Tonight she was there for many reasons, mostly to give heartfelt support and friendship to Dad, both things neither was able to nurture during their marriage. In the past week I had noticed Dad marvel at her change from the old days to the woman she was now — confident, passionate — and as I watched him water her throughout the evening, I saw, as if through his eyes, his happiness and respect for her newfound empowerment. And though I wished in my heart that they would get back together, I knew there was no chance of it.

Finally the music started and Dad asked me if I would like to dance. When I was little, we would dance with me standing on his toes, flying around the room. I was too big for that now, but no one, no boy, had ever danced with me. Up till now, it had only been Deirdre and me gyrating wildly to Elvis records. But now the spotlight was on my father and me, and I was petrified — this would either be the best of the worst moment of my life. As the crowd watched, Mom moving in the closest, I stepped out to meet him on the floor. Once there, I just closed my eyes and prayed.

It went perfectly. Our simple foxtrot was smooth and easy. No tripping, no stepping on toes, just wonderful. His hand rested lightly on my waist, guiding me with all the support and tenderness I had missed from the last seven years without him there to hold me as a father. Though I don't recall if there was actually a spotlight in the room, there may as well have been one illuminating every step of our virtual flight. And through it all, my torturous self-consciousness just melted away like ice under his warm, reassuring gaze.

When the music finally stopped, we were overwhelmed with applause from all sides. I felt high and utterly free as Dad bowed and floated off. He then stepped up to my sister for the next dance. Tight skirts were the craze and Deirdre, used to much more dance-friendly clothes, was in for a surprise. As she tried the simple maneuvers of the trot, I floated back down to earth, taking great sisterly pleasure in watching her struggle and stumble across the floor.

While my mother was on her way to getting drunk, Beverly seemed quiet now. Although she knew the ropes of publicity and how these sorts of parties worked, she was still a teenager and pouted if Dad indulged too long in a conversation that didn't revolve around her. It became very clear to me through the course of the night that Beverly's main objective was to show Dad off to all her friends. Instead of begrudging her for this, I understood. I felt the same way. I always wanted my friends around to show them I actually had a dad; a dad who was somewhere around once in awhile, a dad who was mine, if not perfect.

I sat down next to Beverly and told her that Deirdre and I wouldn't be there much longer. It was close to midnight and I knew Mom was about to send us home. Since they were leaving early the next day for Vancouver, where Dad would part with the Zaca, I wished her a good trip. She told me that they were going to settle up with Pat and start formal divorce proceedings, hoping that soon after they could get married. I took in the news as if she was telling me she was going to try a new shade of nail polish. In my family, divorce was a given. My mother would ultimately marry three times, as would Dad.

Beverly smiled, telling me we could come and stay with them in Jamaica, where they would settle after the wedding. This was fine with me — for Dad to settle anywhere closer than Europe was all I really cared about. We would visit them after Christmas, though this seemed years away. She gave me a kiss and a hug and turned as Mom came over with word that it was time to say our goodbyes. The truth was that I had no one to say anything to except for Dad.

Deirdre had just said goodbye to him, so I reluctantly walked over, dragging my feet every inch of the way, sadness welling up inside with each breath. I hated these moments — goodbyes of any kind. I could never see beyond the dreary sense of finality they always conjured in me.

This was especially true in Dad's case. He was always gone longer than he said he'd be, and then, after he did come home, he'd disappear again just as we got used to a daily routine. The bear hug he gave me when I got over to him, however, made all the mounting emotion subside — at least momentarily. He led me off to an empty table, pulled me onto his lap and I was five years old all over again.

Now alone, he looked me right in the eye with a knowing nod.

"Granny told me about all those wonderful swim meets of yours. I want you to know how incredibly proud of you I am, Slim. Keep it up, Okay?"

I hugged him and told him I loved him and missed him when he was gone. I nuzzled in closer, not wanting to go, and he rested his chin on my head, and we sat like that for what felt like hours.
He finally whispered, "I'll be seeing you at Christmas. You're going to love the horse I picked out for you."
Although horses were Deirdre's thing, I loved them and rode well, too. "He's all black, with a white diamond right in the middle of his forehead and perfect white socks to match."

I focused deeply on a quivering candle in hopes of keeping my tears back, but even so, even without looking up, I sensed the deep aura of melancholy

Dad gave off. His rare vulnerability exposed, a profound sense of sadness now descended, paradoxically uniting us in a completely different place than we had been just minutes earlier on the dance floor.

I pushed aside my desire to find out what was causing it, for fear of breaking this sad but beautiful silence. Wordless, we sat there a bit longer before I sensed him starting to pull back. Again, he told me how much he loved me and hoped we liked Beverly because of how important she was to him. I told him I liked her fine. Just then, a photographer strode past and snapped a picture of us. And just like that, the spell was broken.

"Okay, Slim, time to get to bed. I'll be back in two weeks. It won't be long, time will fly."

Another kiss and hug, during which I whispered how much I really like Beverly. He walked us all to the car and we blew him kisses as we drove off, looking back as he stood waving and smiling.

◆ ◆ • • ◆ • • ◆

It was just ten days later that we were startled from our sleep by someone at the door. Even though the doorbell continued to ring convulsively, no one answered it. Something felt odd. People never showed up to our house without calling first, let alone at 7am.

I finally rolled out of bed, put on some slippers and crept down the stairs where I heard at least two or three voices talking on the other side of the door. Since we were now three females living alone, we had installed a little peephole in the door for just such unexpected occasions.

I twisted the latch, pulled open the tiny door and was instantly blinded by the WHAP of a flashbulb – then another – and another – until I finally made out voices shouting:

"Did you know your dad died?"
"How does it feel?"
"Do you miss him?"
"Had he been ill long?"

And on and on, as I lost feeling everywhere but in my heart, which began pounding with a sense of terror I had never felt before, or since.
Finally, through the blur, I heard my mother running down the stairs behind me. I turned to look at her as she hugged me close.

"Sweetheart, go upstairs to you room. I'll come up in a minute. We'll talk – it'll be okay."

I still heard the voices outside, and the fear, rage and overwhelming sadness continued swirling together, sweeping me up until – I can't believe this is happening. Just a week ago I was in his arms saying goodbye and laughing at how quickly the time would pass before we saw each other again. This is so unfair! – is all I remember hearing, over and over like unending thunder rolling through my throbbing head.

I couldn't believe Deirdre somehow slept on through all this commotion. I don't know how I got to the top of the stairs, but I turned on the landing in time to hear my mother open the door and tell off the gaggle of reporters who has gathered.

She told them all how horrible they were to talk to his child like that, but they didn't seem to hear her. Instead, they started bombarding her with questions. She answered that she had nothing to say except that he will be very much missed and to please let us grieve in peace.

I went into the bathroom and locked the door – my only private place. I sat down on the toilet and cried and cried. I couldn't understand how life could be gone in a moment. Did he suffer? He wasn't alone, was he? How can it be now that we won't ever, ever see him again? Sorrow consumed me. A feeling so deep, it hurt my chest, my brain, every part of my being. I guessed that that was what it felt like to have your heart broken.

A short time later Mom knocked on the door and said, "Honey, when you are ready, come out and we'll talk."

Somehow I concluded that she'd already awoken Deirdre and told her the news. I have never been able to recall just how long I stayed curled up in a ball, or what exactly she said to soothe me when I finally came out of the bathroom, but I do know that on that day my childhood ended.

95

96

Sean in Vietnam

Cooky Debidour
Paris, 2004

We met in Paris in 1962, I was 18, full of life
Studying art and interior architecture
Also a debutante and as so invited to every jet set event
Or cultural happening.

So we met at an English play where we both came with a date
We had friends in common, we talked.
He asked for my telephone number, called me the day after
And we agreed to meet the following day.

He picked me up on his motorbike, so more himself than in his dinner jacket.
We went for a long drive out of the city and had so much fun
We just decided to stay together
And stayed linked until he disappeared in April '70.

At the time we wondered about the meaning of life
And the ways of expressing ourselves,
Our talents, our beliefs, it was the Age of Aquarius.
We were not hippies but certainly utopists
We wanted to be part of our times and they were changing!

Life was fascinating and we had lots of fun.

We both traveled for our work.
I had become a model so to be free and meet him around the world
We would always manage to meet.

We deeply cared for each other but we had so much to discover.
We both were honest for the meaningful things in life
It once brought us apart for several months.

I was a minor and my father had forbidden Sean to approach me
And I didn't know.
Through his mother he contacted me, we met and he proposed to marry me
I told him there would always be time for that.

I was wrong.

He disliked profoundly that most of the people regarded him as his father's son
And wanted badly to be offered a chance to show his skills,
Act in a really good movie.
On the screen he had a very strong presence and the potential of a star
But he needed to be offered the opportunity of being revealed and recognized.

The movies did not bring him that.
He also needed action
He discovered an interest in taking pictures
He made his first test shots and made beautiful shots
He then wouldn't stop taking pictures.
He would go on acting, but being less and less interested
And he would photograph his surroundings wherever he went.
And that brought him to Vietnam from Singapour where he was on location
For a French movie called "Cinq Gars á Singapour."

I didn't mention that he was a strikingly good-looking man,
Very tall with an archangelic face.

I not often have seen a man that without trying or wanting
Attract people so naturally.
Time changed him and made him look every time more interesting
As he would grow into himself.

He was always questioning himself on the meanings of life.
He had an immense appetite for life and loved to read
About politics, technology, psychology, wilderness,
Any subject he could reflect on.
When we were apart, we would write, so I have lots of letters from all over.
He asked me to join him in Vietnam but I refused
I hated this war and any war and wouldn't dream of going there even with him.

He became a war photographer in Vietnam, informing the world
Of what was going on.
He would do it well.

He wrote telling me how he felt and what was going on
He also covered "la Guerre des 6 Jours."

We would always meet
At a point he was sending me all his work
That I then had developed and would give to UPI in Paris.

I can say he was a solitaire and needed privacy
To reflect on himself and on life.
The tragedy of war affected him and at times
He would have terrible nightmares
But the adrenalin of action
And strong and deep friendship of other war photographers
Became addictive.

Not long before he disappeared, he wanted me to go with him to Bali
And to stay.
His best friend Tim Page had been horribly wounded
And he suddenly needed to get out of it,
But life is strange.
He stayed and he was later convinced to go on his last trip
Although by then he realized how life is precious and easy to lose.

Although he died so young I still say to myself he achieved a short
But fulfilled life.
And he left the world the stunning pictures he took.

I have been asked before to write about Sean and never wanted to.
Now, Rory, you have asked me to and I realize I have been living near Sean,
A part of his evolution nobody could talk about.
He could have lost himself in so many facile illusions,
He faced bravely his wonders and his tragic destiny
He was the most attaching man
I will love him always.

I have shared for the last 25 years the life of a man I love dearly,
The father of the 21-year-old daughter I adore
But Sean will remain in my heart till I die.

From what he had been telling me, and from what I know about him
I am sure that he tried his best to remain alive throughout his captivity
And face Death like being part of All Things
There is obviously so much more to say about him...

Sean was born on the 31st of Mai 1941 and disappeared on the 6th of April 1970.

George Hamilton Remembers Sean Flynn

Sean and I met in traffic court. He'd wrecked a motorcycle and I was arrested for speeding. They didn't accuse me of being drunk, but I was. We were both arraigned in court on the same day. I was about two years older than Sean — seventeen at the time — and he was about fifteen. He'd had this motorcycle accident. He didn't get hurt, but he was in court, and I was in court, so we sat there and started talking.

We were both out of an automobile and didn't have anyway of getting anywhere. And we were both very much into trying to date girls. Of course, you can't date a girl on a bicycle. So Sean and I came up with the idea that if I got a car, we would search for girls who could drive. In fact, that was our first question to them: can you drive?

Sean kept talking about acting, he was doing some play in school. Now, two years makes a lot of difference at that age, and he was just sort of experimenting with the idea of becoming an actor. I'd had the lead in a few plays in Palm Beach and had decided that I wanted to go to Hollywood, so we talked about that.
He talked about doing some really adventuresome things, and you could feel his father's influence. He seemed to be really reckless, but I think it was more that he just had an utter disregard for danger. I remember we got on a boat and left for Cuba once, right after the fall of Havana. It was just a rowboat, and we were going to row there. Of course we only got a few miles out to sea. These kinds of ideas came from Sean. He seemed reckless, but at the same time there was a great, sweet quality about him — he was a very, very likable person.

In those days Sean was also like a caged animal. Life was coming upon him very fast. I had the feeling that he was just ready to explode. I think he had read all these things his father had done and wanted to out-do them. There was an impatience in him, as though time was running faster for him.

Sean and I saw a lot of each other in Palm Beach. He always had a sort of begrudging humor, with a half-smile on his face, about my exploits, as we talked about what I was going to do and what he was going to do. We had some different attitudes about things.

That summer I went to work in New York, at a beach club. I had told Sean I was going to Hollywood after the summer — that I was just going to go. Meantime he went to Lawrenceville.

Then one day I got a call from him saying that his father was in New York, at a party at the Gabors' on 64th Street, and that his father wanted him to come up from school and go to dinner with him and could I get him a date! So I got one of these wonderful little girls from the right family, with a circle pin and everything. I suggested that they meet.

I got the girl to come over and the next thing I know it's 9pm, then 10pm, and still no Sean. The girl's mother called, asking if her daughter was all right, and finally at 11 o'clock Sean called to say that he had a little problem. I said, Sean, I've got this girl waiting, and I've been covering for you.

He said, well, I'm at El Morocco. I said, El Morocco, what the hell are you doing there?

Dad wanted me to come meet him here, he said, so why don't you come over now? El Morocco was for older people, so I decided to take the girl home first. I dropped her off and then went.

When I got there Sean was dressed in a corduroy jacket, white bucks and a buttoned-down shirt. Errol was in a gray pinstripe suit, with a cigarette holder in his hand, and standing with his young girlfriend Beverly Aadland and her mother.

I also noticed a 35-year-old 'semi-pro' that Errol had gotten for Sean as a date. Sean was acting like the perfect gentleman, lighting her cigarettes and standing every time she stood. He was the only one doing this and I have to admit that to me at the time it seemed a travesty to watch.

Errol had this wonderful style about him that made you think he was standing when he wasn't. And Sean continued to play the gentleman as he pulled her chair out for this hooker. So I sat down, and noticed that Errol was drinking an awful amount of vodka. It was in 1957.

I went to Hollywood after that, and did see Errol a couple more times at parties both in New York and in L.A. He had a sort of retinue of guys — one was a bone specialist to the stars, another had owned a night club called the Hag. Errol was in bad shape then and these guys all sort of propped each other up when they went out clubbing.

I remember one night I was up at a party at Hugh O'Brien's house up on Mulholland. Errol showed up and someone said, It's Errol Flynn! and in came this entourage of people that looked like Elvis Presley's group. They were all dressed in black and whooping it up.

Errol still had this enormous charisma about him at the time, enormous style. No matter how bad things were, he was still intact. I remember that he had just been doing the play, "Jane Eyre." He wouldn't learn his lines and Huntington Hartford was mad. Hunt had the terrible ability to always pick the wrong project to do —

he had no business sense and if you gave him money, he lost it.

But Hunt wanted to do the play and he wanted Errol. Apparently, Errol needed some cash to pay off back taxes. I think he ended up using a teleprompter, but the play was a shambles, anyway.

Sean and I then lost touch for about a year. I had come out to Hollywood and within a few months, well, I was lucky, I got in movies and never stopped working. In my third movie, *WHERE THE BOYS ARE*, we went to shoot in Florida and, of course, the first guy I see on the beach is Sean. He said, Jesus, you're in the movies already? This is terrific!

I told him it was simple. He said, really? I said yeah, and then we took over Fort Lauderdale for the movie.

We got all these high school kids to be extras. Joe Pasternak was producing. There were thousands of girls — the movie was packed with girls — and Sean loved the whole package. He said to me, gee, I don't understand — first you went to Hollywood and now you have all these girls knocking on your dressing room door, and they're in your bed at the hotel, they're everywhere! This is the greatest thing I've ever seen, and you know something? This is what I am really meant to do!

I said, you should be an actor, so I went to Joe Pasternak and said can you put this guy in the picture? So, when you watch the film, there is a scene where there's a guy throwing a football, on the beach, in a blue sweatshirt. That's Sean. There was a girl with enormous tits and Sean insisted on being next to her during the filming.

We had some great adventures at that time. Sean said to me, I'm coming to Hollywood! And I said, when you do, you will have already made your first picture, so just look me up and I'll help you.

When he finally arrived, he had nowhere to stay. I had a Rolls Royce that I had rented and was living in an apartment on Sweetzer in West Hollywood. My agent was Hy Seeger. When he met Sean, Hy said, Jesus, what a good-looking guy. I said, yeah, he could be an actor right away, don't you think? Sean and Hy got along immediately, so Hy said he would like to handle Sean.

One day I told Sean I was leaving town to do a film and that he could stay in my new apartment that I had just gotten at Sunset Towers. Please, though, I said. Do me a favor. Don't do anything bad because I want to continue to live here.

Next thing I knew, I read in the paper that he had shot off a flare-gun and burnt up the apartment with Tuesday Weld. It cost me an enormous fee in damages and Sean said he was sorry.

Next thing I knew, he met Harry Joe Brown, who wanted to put him in *SON OF CAPTAIN BLOOD*. So they went to Jack Mahoney, a great stuntman, with whom Errol had worked. Sean begins pumping iron and putting on a lot of weight.

Sean started driving around Sunset in this Jag he bought wearing a hat like d'Artagnan's. It was a huge hat with a large plume sticking out of the side. I told Sean that he'd better get insurance on that car but he just shrugged me off. Of course, the next week he drove it into a telephone pole and totaled it.

Over many late nights Sean and I stayed up and talked philosophy. Sean's philosophy was totally different from mine, although I have to say that now mine is more like his was back then. He had the attitude that he didn't give a shit, he didn't care, why worry, just go for it. I'd tell him I don't see any need to do all that, I want to be in pictures in a nice, romantic lead, where I don't have to fight anything or anybody. Sean wanted to fight, wanted to fence – he was looking for the adventurous thing.

We thought differently about many things. I told him that I didn't need to go around flexing or getting my nose broken a couple times. He would say that it doesn't matter. We sat up night after night talking about what we wanted to do with our lives. I would say I love driving my Rolls Royce and Sean would say I don't want to drive a Rolls Royce. I would say, well, it's just my style.

Time passed, and I was off making movies. He was making movies, too, in Spain. Then he went off to Africa, became a 'white hunter' and contracted malaria in the process. He was out in the bush a lot, and he had many close calls with both animals and the elements.

He also had an apartment in Paris that his grandmother had left him. He spent a lot of time there and loaded it down with leopard skins, tiger skins, and rifles all over the walls. Sean started really liking Paris, as well as Madrid.

I went to a gym one day in Madrid and there he was, so we started talking. I asked him how it was going and he said great. There were a bunch of guys on this film – Ty Hardin, Steve Reeves, Gordon Scott – and we just had some incredible evenings in Madrid.

Sean had just finished a film and was then the 'darling' of Paris. He spoke French without an accent and all the girls loved him because he used their slang, all these expressions. He was living at the Hotel Balman on the Rive Gauche, in a little room, and I would pile in there whenever I came to town. Sean told me about Africa and the adventures he'd had. He thought Paris was a little too civilized but he also liked the bohemian quality about it. Madrid was where movies were happening, also in Rome, but he didn't get into that scene.

Then I met Sean's girlfriend, Cookie. She seemed to care deeply about Sean and was always asking me questions about him. I could tell she worried about him. I think she was in love with him.

A few years later, when I was in London, Sean called me. He said that he and his pal Dana Stone were coming through from Vietnam, and that they had just been with John Steinbeck and did I want to go out and have some laughs. I said great. He came to the hotel and brought Tim Page with him, who was completely berserk – I mean totally out of his head. We were in an elevator together and I found myself just staring at his head with all his shrapnel wounds.

Tim had a steel plate on one side of his head. He'd been shot by everybody while he was covering the war like Sean, with a camera for UPI. Well, I thought, here were two crazy guys who didn't give a shit, just out of Saigon. And here I was with my little dinner jacket, trying to be cool. Here I was with two guys who wanted to carry weapons through the lobby.

We were in a car and when it backfired, they both hit the ground. I couldn't believe it. Sean said, hey, you don't know where we just came from. We don't ask anymore, about getting a taxi, we just put a .45 to their head and tell them where we want to go.

One night the manager of the hotel came up – he had heard noises – and there was Sean in Viet-Cong pajamas with blood all over them. He had a flag in the room and a whole footlocker full of souvenirs; Sean loved to shock you with this stuff. And Page was like a hummingbird on Benzedrine — it was a bizarre time.

That night I went to a gambling casino called The Pair of Shoes, owned by Eric Steiner. I asked for credit, which they gave me, and proceeded to win 20 to 30 thousand pounds with Sean and four Italian playboys. Sean looked at me and said, is it always like this? and I said, only in the movies.

So, as we went up to the cage to get our money, I said to Sean, we must do something extraordinary with this money, and he agreed. Sean said we should go somewhere we have never been and I said yeah; let's think it over at the hotel.

Well, the guy wouldn't pay us, saying he'd been busted by an Arab. So when we realized he wasn't going to pay us, we got a little heavy with him and he brought his dog out that jumped on the crap table. So I said to the guy, meet us at the hotel and we will straighten this out. Later, as Sean and I sit and wait, Sean says, so, what shall we do, grind him into paint?

I said, wait a minute, Sean, we'll just get the money. So the guy arrived and I say, listen, pal, I know a lot of people like Hedda Hopper and Louella Parsons, and all the Americans won't want to come here if you don't pay up.

He suggested that we go to the casino in Beirut where we would get the rest of our money — he'd given us half and the next thing I knew we were on a flight to Beirut. I had been seeing the President's daughter, Lucy Johnson, at the time, and it was all over the papers. It must have been 1967. Sean had been in Vietnam for about two years at that time.

The age for the draft was nineteen, and I was too old at twenty-six, but they wanted to make an example out of me because I was dating the President's daughter. Sean had gotten out of the draft because of his malaria, but I had a lot of heat on me.

We arrived in Beirut and asked for the Presidential suite at the best hotel. We got it and it was huge. We lay down to get some sleep and the next thing I knew a beautiful girl was knocking on the door saying, I represent the Red Cross on behalf of the United Arab Republic and we would like for you to give blood.

I said to the girl, look, I'm fresh out of blood but there is another guy in the next room that loves to give. Let me go get him for you. So I got Sean up and he said yes, shit, we'll do it! He asked how much they needed and she said a pint each and a picture of you each. There is a false teaching here that only fat people can give blood, so if they see thin people give it, it will help.

At 6pm we showed up at the Red Cross center in Beirut. As we were walking up the steps to the building, I turned to Sean and said, how the hell did you get us into this? And he just said, well, it's good for our image to do things like this.

There were at least 80 newspapers and 65 photographers so Sean announces Mr. Hamilton and I wanted to give blood to show our true spirit for the fighting man. And so I ask that my blood, and Mr. Hamilton's, not be given to just one fighting man, but rather we'd like to give a drop to each fighting man.

I looked at him and said are you a crazed person. I'll never forget that. So as not to be outdone, I said, those of you who want to photograph this for your newspapers, will have to give blood as well, or we won't allow you in.

Well, about 40 photographers went in to give blood and the press loved it. It made a great story. They gave us a huge red cross. I said to Sean, you know I will never be able to work in Hollywood again after giving blood to the Arabs.

Anyway, when we went in to give blood, they first handed us a list of health questions. When Sean admitted to having had malaria, they said, sorry, we can't take your blood. So in the end Sean got out of it and I was the only one to give blood.

We then were minor celebrities in Beirut, and so we'd go to the St. George Hotel all day long and these beautiful girls with hair growing out of their nostrils would ask us questions. Sean found this Israeli girl – I don't know how he found her in Beirut – but he bought a machine gun off her, a Thompson .45.

I suggested that this is not the place to have a machine gun, but he said he bought it for when he went back to Vietnam. He said there were only two things that were of value there: a gold Rolex and a gun.

That night we went to the casino to get our money, but the guy just laughed at us. In any case, I felt lucky, so I started to place a bet when I noticed Sean leaning against the teller window and looking sick. He said it was from the day's experience at the blood bank, and I reminded him that he didn't give any blood. He said it was just from being around it.

And that's what really endeared me to Sean was after all these macho kinds of things – he did he still got sick at the sight of blood. So in the casino there was a big Arab who said he would cover any bets I made and, amazingly, I won another 30,000 and the next thing I know about eight Arabs stood up and said, you are our guests in Beirut, anything you want, you will have no problem in Beirut. First thing Sean asked for was hashish. I said Sean, you had better be careful and he said, it's okay in Saigon.

So there was Sean, putting hashish in a cigarette, loading it like a missile, and eight Arabs. We went to the mountains with them where they gave a party for us and there were all these girls, 'white slaves', from the Blue Bells in London. These poor girls would come over to us and whisper please, please, can you help us get a passport, we want to get out of here. And Sean is saying, not to worry, I will have you all liberated. But the place was lined with bodyguards.

Then the wife came home and everyone seemed to scatter. In came this little wife, with a furry little chin and three children. Our host seemed terrified. We stayed in Beirut for a few more days and had a great adventure before returning to London.

Tim Page once told me that nobody wanted to be around Flynn. He told me that Sean would go out on a 'search and destroy' mission and that he would jump out of the helicopter in a bright red shirt and blue jeans. Everybody had the feeling that he was going to get it. The other guys would be crawling on their stomachs but Sean would stand up tall and charge in.

That was when I knew I hadn't been wrong about Sean's disregard for danger. Anyway, we are flying back and Sean is up in the front with the pilots and I say to him let's go back to London and get the rest of our money. We really made a killing and we should go back and do something exciting with it.

Sean said, no, no, no. I want to go back to Vietnam. I said are you crazy, you are an old man back there. Why do you want to go back, you've done it, people know it, what's the purpose?

He said George, you don't understand – it's the only place in the world where there is something happening. His exact words. Sean said he wanted to do what Michael Raye did. Sean had read this book of Michael Raye's, who had been captured by the North Vietnamese and had seen the war from the other side, in Hanoi.

I now think that Sean wanted to get captured and have a similar experience for himself. I once met a Swedish correspondent from Amsterdam, who said that he'd seen Sean after his capture and that he needed medicine for his malaria. He said that they were moving him around a lot, too, to different field hospitals.

I was at the White House when I heard of his capture in Cambodia. I got it the minute it came in on the wire service. President Johnson had asked me what I wanted for my birthday, so now I told him that I would like to get as much information on Sean Flynn as I could. It made me think back to when Sean had gotten hit in the past and had gone into a field hospital, I think because a Claymore mine had exploded near him. Sean had rambled on and on about elephants, about the knowledge that an elephant has about his own death.

Eventually, Sean and I had went our own separate ways, and he formed his own life. When our paths crossed, we were dramatically opposed to each other on a lot of issues.

I am now more like he was then. Now I don't give a shit, but then I did. I think he would have mellowed and I think he could have become a good actor if he had wanted. I think he was trying to get the macho-chauvinistic thing down, so he couldn't be faulted on that. And the vulnerable side that he didn't show would emerge later.

The last time I saw him, he had just gotten onto a plane in Geneva on his way to Vietnam. In Palm Beach Sean was a sweet rebellious kid and at the same time a real hellion.

His mother Lili came to me several times after Sean disappeared to see if she could find out anything. It really took a toll on her, like she had been in a battle. Sean had a humor about him. Like Errol, he was mischievous and teasing, but he also had this tender vulnerable side that was almost childlike, and that I never saw leave him. In the end I thought that he had been locked into a role he had to play, but that he was slowly becoming the man he really was — not somebody's else's son, just a man named Sean Flynn.

Michael Herr

One of Sean's fellow war correspondents was Michael Herr. Herr is the author of "Dispatches," his award-winning account of the war in Vietnam, from which this passage is quoted.

"Flynn was cleaning his camera lens with a length of Australian sweat scarf that he always wore in the field, but the least movement sent up a fine-grained dust that seemed to hang there without re-settling, giving the light a greasy quality and caking in the corners of your eyes. The Marines were looking hard at Flynn and you could see that he was blowing their minds, the way he blew minds all over Vietnam.

"He was indeed the son of Captain Blood, but that didn't mean much to the grunts, since most of them, the young ones, had barely ever heard of Errol Flynn. It was just apparent to anyone who looked at him that he was what the Marines would call "a dude who definitely had his shit together."

"I had been in 'Nam the better half of a year now, and we all nearly young enough to be mistaken for grunts ourselves, but Flynn was special. We all had our movie-fed fantasies, the Marines, too, and it could be totally disorienting to have this outrageously glamorous figure intrude on them, really unhinging, like looking up to see that you've been sharing a slit trench with John Wayne. But you got used to that part of Flynn quickly.

"Sean Flynn could look even more incredibly beautiful than his father Errol had thirty years before as Captain Blood, but sometimes he looked more like Artaud coming out of some heavy heart-of-darkness trip, overloaded on information — the input! The input!

"He'd give off a bad sweat and sit for hours, combing his moustache through with the saw blade of his Swiss Army knife. When he first arrived in Vietnam in the summer of '65, he had been considered news himself, and a lot of stories were written about his early trips into combat.

"Most of them managed to include all the clichés, all of them calling him "swashbuckling." There were still a lot of easy things to say about him, and a lot of people around who were more than willing to say them, but after you knew him all of that talk just depressed you.

"There were a number of serious (heavy) journalists who could not afford to admit that anyone who looked as good as Flynn looked could possibly have anything more going for him. They chose not to take him as seriously as they took themselves (which was fine with Sean), and they accused him of coming to Vietnam to play, as though the war was like Africa had been for him, or the South of France or one of the places he had gone to make those movies that people were always judging him by.

"But there were a lot of people playing in Vietnam, more than the heavies cared to admit, and Flynn's playing was done only on the most earnest levels. He wasn't much different from the rest; he was deeply fascinated by war, by this war, but he admitted it, knew where he stood in it, and he behaved as though it was nothing to be ashamed of.

"It gave him a vision of Vietnam that was profound, black and definitive, a knowledge of its wildness, that very few of his detractors would have understood. All of this was very obvious in his face, particularly the wildness, but those people only saw it as handsome, making you realize that as a group, newspapermen were not necessarily any more observant or imaginative than accountants.

"Flynn move on and found his friends among those who never asked him to explain himself, among the GIs and the Apaches of the press corps, and he established his own celebrity there. (There would be occasional intrusions: embarrassingly deferential information officers, or a run-in with Colonel George Patton, Jr., who put him through one of those my-father-knew-your-father trials.)

"The grunts were always glad to see him. They'd called him "Seen," a lot of them, and tell him that they'd caught one of his flicks on R&R in Singapore of Taiwan, something that only a grunt could bring up and get away with, since all of that was finished for Flynn, the dues paying and accommodations, and he didn't like to talk about it.

"Sometime during his years in Vietnam, he realized that there really were people whom he cared for and could trust, it must have been a gift he never expected to have, and it made him someone who his father, on the best day he ever had, could have envied."

When I became a mother, a friend whom I hadn't seen a few years asked me what I had named my son. I said, "Sean."

"Of course," was her reply. "And did this help you give up the ghost?"

The tone of her voice revealed the sarcasm, and it became quite clear to me then that both friends and family had wearied of my obsession with a brother lost. It definitely suggested to me that over the years I had been a burden to other with my crusade, my quest for information. At the time I was shocked to realized that I had become obsessed, but still couldn't seem to get any answers.

For two decades I had dealt with government agencies, rascals, rogues, do-gooders and mystics, with anyone, in fact, offering the flimsiest hint that my brother had survived his capture by the communists on that jungle road in Cambodia in April of 1970. It took many years to reconcile myself to accepting the inevitable, the reality and finality of death.

The truth was hard to accept, that there had been so many moments of promise during my extended search. The missing-prisoners-of-war associations, for example, who gathered reports from behind enemy lines. They were helpful.

There were middle-of-the-night calls from interested parties, who may have read about Sean and others and had secret sources from whom to glean valuable information. Some of these out-of-the-night individuals were sincere in their intentions, but were sadly limited in producing results. Others told of planned incursions into Laos and Cambodia, where they insisted Sean and his fellow captive Dana Stone were recently sighted.

One of these was an IRA fugitive, who said he was certain of the exact location of Sean's then current prison encampment. He even brought me a fingerprint that he said belonged to Sean, but I couldn't find a match for it. This was fifteen years after my brother's capture, but still they all insisted they could deliver dramatic results if only their missions could be financed.

Several of these interested parties seemed to really believe what they professed to know. Others were likely nothing but scam artists, whose only goal was the money they could extract from the relatives of the missing. I hate to think how many good families were cheated out of their savings in this manner. I would have been among them, had I the finances.

As it was, I did invest a lot. I sent for information through the Freedom of Information Act and for the FBI reports and the belongings of Sean's that were sent and stored at different friends' homes. I tracked and chased every clue to his life. There were frustrating flares of hope that would occasionally brighten the horizon: a word here, a news item there, a phone call of a chance meeting with one of his old buddies.

And all the time, the truth was, in my heart I never knew if I was of ever could be doing enough in my search. Was he somewhere out there alive in some prison camp, waiting for one of his sisters to rescue him?

Eventually the U.S. State Department provided information that began, finally, to dim my optimism. Through the Freedom of Information Act I was eventually issued the following U.S Air Force report:

"A wrap-up of information provided by two ralliers on sighting and execution in June of 1971 of two U.S. journalists in Tapeo area, Krocr Chhmar District, Kampon Cham Province. The journalists were executed on orders of Ya Sabol, KC chief of Krocr Chhmar District. Reference E. was DIA's evaluation that information probably equated to S. Flynn and D. Stone, both U.S. journalists captured on April 6, 1970 in Svay Rieng Province, Cambodia."

If the date was accurate, and the information correct, it meant that Sean and Dana only survived fifteen months after their capture. At the time, Sean was 30 years old.

Sean Leslie Thompson Flynn was but a year old when his mother, French actress Lili Damita, filed for divorce from his father Errol.

Lili and Errol had met in 1934 while crossing the Atlantic on the passenger steamship the S.S. Paris, then the transatlantic pride of the French Line. Errol, dashingly handsome in his Saville Row suits and Dover street black white shoes, was on his way from London to Hollywood at the request of Jack Warner, who wanted the young actor to screen test at his Burbank studio for a job that paid $75 a week.

Lili Damita was already a famous film star who had played opposite most of the leading male stars. A stormy but talented French actress, Lili herself was on her way to a contract in Hollywood with Sam Goldwyn, and Errol, who described her as one of the most beautiful women in the world, was swept away by the dark-haired beauty in the silk, skin-hugging dresses as she promenaded along the decks.

Once her initial standoffishness was melted by Errol's cool charm, they met again in Manhattan, and then again on a Beverly Hills tennis court. She asked him to share her bungalow and he accepted. They both seemed totally infatuated with one another. Within weeks they flew off to Arizona to get married. Though they left the chapel hand in hand, it wasn't long, however, before their tempestuous relationship led to constant squabbles over the smallest of details: his love of oysters, her buying sprees. Beyond that, there were constant intense gazes and suggestive invitations from beautiful people around them who seemed bent on tearing them apart.

After a trial separation, Lili contacted Errol and asked for a reconciliation. They reunited briefly, and Lili soon after victoriously announced to him that she was pregnant.

By CAPTAIN BLOOD, Lili realized that their marriage was doomed. When it became clear at the film's premiere that his star was rising, the aging silent film actress broke down, sobbing, "I've lost him forever." Soon, the couple moved to separate quarters. Tired of the explosive marriage, Errol moved in with his good friend, David Niven. Lili, taking baby Sean, moved to a house on Rodeo Drive, several blocks away.

Divorce finally came in April, 1941. Growing tired of Hollywood, she moved to Palm Beach, Florida, where her prospects for a new life and a new husband looked more promising. Dad built his bachelor home, Mulholland Farm, in the Hollywood Hills.

The first time Sean came to spend the summer with us, he was seven years old.

It was definitely in Sean's nature to get into trouble, or at least to get caught at it. He was a spirited lover of mischief.

One Sunday afternoon, while listening to "The Jack Benny Show" on the radio, Sean sketched out small animal traps. A Boy Scout friend came over to help him create and set the traps as the boys set their sights on the small rabbits who would steal into the yard to chew up my grandmother's garden. The boys never caught any rabbits, so when he spied a bear trap on a film set one day, he asked the prop man about it.

The prop man happily gave it to Sean and the young boy quickly had it put into the trunk of the car for later.

Back at home, Sean strategically placed the bear trap in the driveway leading up to the house, and retreated to hidden vantage point nearby to watch. He didn't have long to wait, as moments later a large, chauffeur-driven limousine arrived and slowly made its way up to the house. Gossip columnist Hedda Hopper was arriving to have lunch with my mother and father.

The chauffeur, thinking it was a toy, avoided the trap by mere inches. A starchy looking gentleman, he straightened his cap before stepping out of the car. Brushing by the trap, he set it off and it snapped shut, catching his trousers. The poor man shrieked, his eyes darting about as he realized he might have to protect Ms. Hopper from all sorts of diabolical plots, but my father quickly arrived, all apologies and charm as he escorted Ms. Hopper into the house and shot a glance at Sean over his shoulder, a glance that meant he would be dealt with later.

Later, from the solitary confinement of his room, Sean watched my father render the bear trap harmless and throw it away. After the lecture on dangerous things, Sean was made to explain his conduct in a letter of apology to Ms. Hopper.

A few days later, however, my father told Sean that he had a surprise for him. In moments, we heard the unmistakable sound of a helicopter as it landed on the lawn. Sean, eight years old at the time, climbed aboard for his first helicopter ride as he accompanied my father across the valley to the studio.

Sean spent a lot of time with my father at the studio. He enjoyed watching my father work, as well as well as the camaraderie my father enjoyed with the crew and stuntmen. Sean would sit in my father's canvas-backed chair with his name printed on it, and watch, fascinated, the endless procession of takes and re-takes.

The crew liked Sean, too, and taught him some of the tricks of the trade. At the studio, for example, Sean first learned how to hold a fencing foil and climb a rope. One day, the young boy even got to duel with a midget stand-in stuntman.

In the quiet of his library, Errol imbued in his son an early sense of adventure with colorful tales of travel to different, exotic parts of the world. Sean never tired to hearing my father's exciting stories of manning a machine gun in 1937 with the Loyalists in the Spanish Civil War, or the rough and tumble life running a copra farm in the wilds of New Guinea.

One day, Sean would grow up to have just as many adventures — becoming a game warden in Africa, living the Bohemian life of a fashion photographer in Paris, and witnessing the Vietnam War firsthand as a photojournalist for five years.

The barn at Mulholland Farm looked like it belonged in Dodge City, a ramshackle structure sitting among oak trees at the base of the property. There Dad kept his two horses: Onyx, his favorite, and Brownie, the pony that belonged to my sister. Sean would spend time there, brushing and feeding the horses with the keeper who would talk about his rodeo days and teach Sean how to care for horses.

Sean would also spend a lot of time in the hayloft. From this vantage point, he could see all the property in the front and often fire off his cap gun in an imaginary battle with rustlers and other desperadoes. Toward the end of that second summer, my father told us that he was on hiatus from the studio, that he would allot each child some special time, and that he was taking Sean, first of all, to a cabin on Lake Mead for a weekend of fishing, just father and son.

It proved to be one of Sean's most delightful memories of his father that began as they drove out across the desert in Dad's Packard. At Lake Mead they registered under false names in order to ensure their privacy. Out on the lake that weekend they caught up on Sean's past year at school and everything of importance to my brother at the time.

It became clear that my father was pleased that Sean wasn't growing up a "momma's boy," but that he had, in fact, quite a bit of spunk. Sean was strong-willed and Dad liked that. They didn't return from the weekend with any fish, but Sean retained the memory of that trip for years.

The last night at the cabin, my father brought out a special gift for Sean: a smooth, polished, the pump-action BB carbine, the one with which he would later accidentally shoot his grandmother.

Back at Mulholland, looking out the barn window, Sean imagined that was the sole survivor of an Indian attack in a fort overrun by the enemy, as two Indian braves (Deirdre and myself) dashed by the window yelping and firing mop handles at him. Sean mouthed the words "Bang, bang" as he sighted along the barrel.

This game continued for another hour and, in a last effort to defend the fort, he backed the two braves up against a library wall and aimed once again. This time a shot missed Dierdre by less than an inch and embedded itself into the wall.

My sister pretended she was hit, and — slowly and dramatically, I might add, a Flynn to the last — slumped and slid down the wall, clutching at her heart and softly moaning. Sean, falling for her act and believing he had hit her, paled in fright, until he was revived by her miraculous recovery in gales of laughter.

114

Almost every other weekend my father would take us to Catalina for the weekend, where he had a slip always waiting for him. The Zaca would be crammed with food, toy and Sean's pirate gear. The ocean was filled with porpoises and the sails would balloon out with the soft offshore wind.

Again, Sean was the right age to absorb and to enjoy all that Dad had to give, and to teach. He learned all about boats that summer and the summers to follow. As we sailed throughout the day, I remember Sean standing close to my father. As we motored into Avalon harbor, the water was often unusually calm and the fog would lift. The setting sun was like a jewel floating off in the distance.

CBS NEWS
A Division of Columbia Broadcasting System, Inc.
Saigon Bureau
Hotel Caravelle
Saigon, Vietnam
Telephones: 90085, 93704 (ext. 206)

August 19, 1970

Dear Mrs. Loomis,

My husband, Dana Stone, was captured in Cambodia with Sean. They have been friends for five years, and I have known Sean for three. At the time Dana and Sean went to Cambodia, we were sharing an apartment in Saigon. Sean had just returned a few ~~dddd~~ weeks before from Bali, and was planning to pack up his belongings here and go back to Bali. He was sidetracked by the Cambodian situation. I do not have any idea how much Time Magazine told you, or whether they have been keeping you informed on the situation of the captured journalists; if they have not been in touch with you regularly, you should call Mr. Murry Gart, Chief of Correspondents for Time/Life in New York. I will tell you what I know, and please, if you have any questions I might be able to answer, just send me a letter.

I am very happy that Dana and Sean were captured together; they are good friends, they both know a great deal about how to take care of themselves in a military situation, they are both strong and well and I know they can adapt to anything that is neccessary. Please do not believe all the trash that was written in Time/Newsweek about them, or their supposed "riding around the war zone on motorbikes". They are both very level headed and did not go out to be captured. This has been implied many times, but it is not true. I was in Cambodia the day they started out on their trip. The road was safe, and their only intention was to go toward the border and maybe get pictures of the US bombing inside Cambodia, which the US was denying at that point. I am nearly 100% positive they were captured alive, and from all reports, all the journalists who have been taken have been treated very well. About two weeks after their capture, Zalin Grant, a friend of theirs who used to be with Army Intelligence, came to Saigon to see if he could dig up any information about them. At this time, about six caucasian journalists had been captured, so it was diffucult to distinguish one from the other, since to the Cambodians, we all look alike. But because Sean is taller than all the others captured, and had on Bermuda shorts, he stood out. There was one report of Four Caucasians and two "Chinese" (probably Japanese) seen about three weeks after Sean and Dana were captured. One of the caucasians fit Sean's description well enough that I am convinced that it was him. From the descriptions of the others I could not tell if Dana was with him. This means that Sean is probably Alive and well, for it would only be the first few hours that would be dangerous; once they were with an officer they would be in no danger. Now there is nothing to do but wait.

As you know, three journalists were released. I talked to all three about their expiorences, and they were very well treated. They got plenty to eat, were not bound except at first, and their captors were very concerned with their safety...even to risking their own lives to protect them. These three felt they were released because their political views could easily be established ~~and~~ through their previous articles (this is more diffucult to do with photographers) and that one of them was a woman. They were also always kept with Cambodian troops (pro-Sihanouk); as you know, the North Vietnamese and NLF do not admit their presence in Cambodia, so any pleas for information about the journalists has to go through Sihanouk and his followers.

Everything I have done for Dana I have done for Sean as well. At first, in Cambodia, I was able to contact the North Vietnamese and NLF Delegates to ask them to help me gain information about Dana and Sean. I asked them to use their influence with Sihanouk

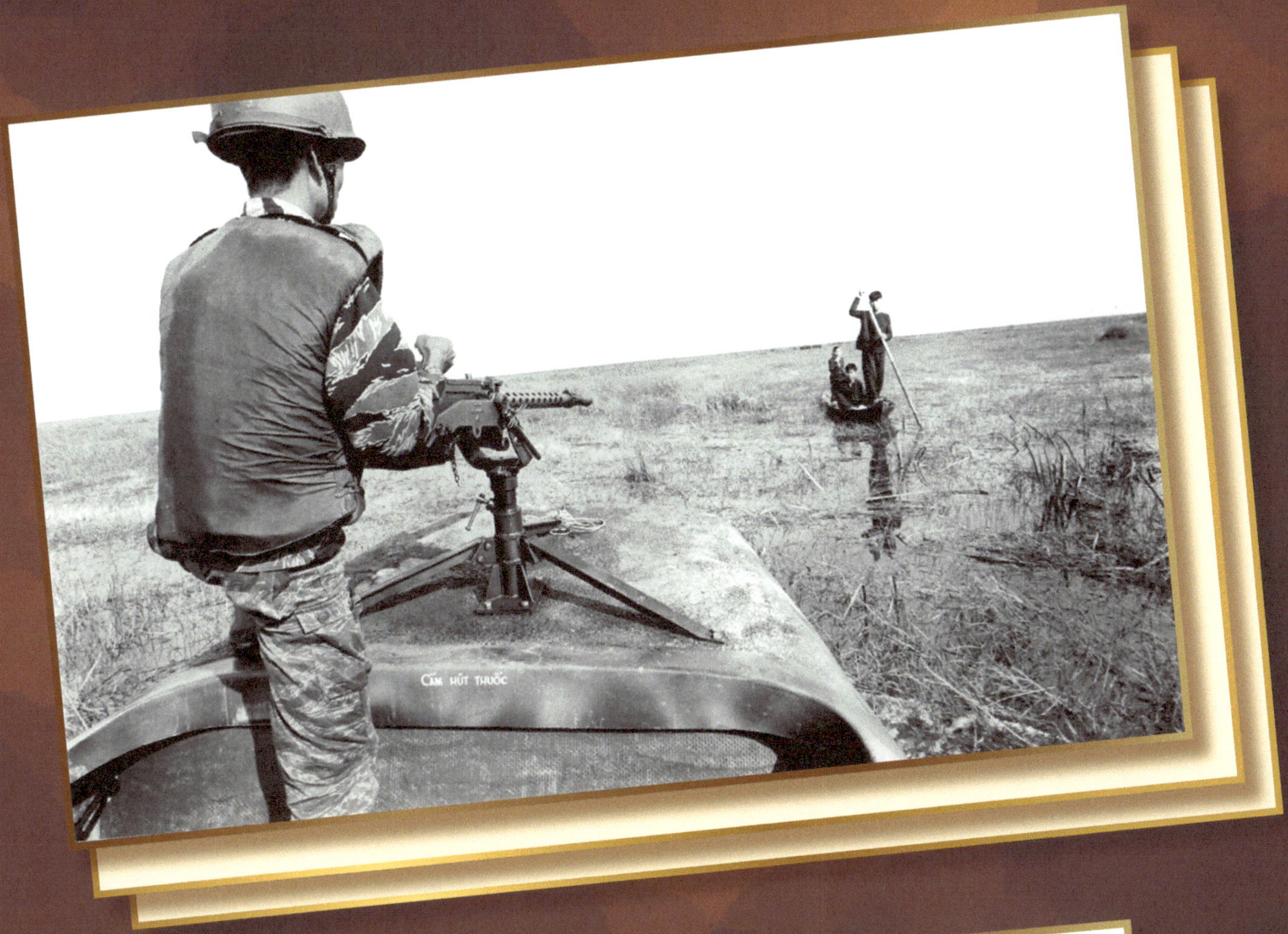
CẤM HÚT THUỐC

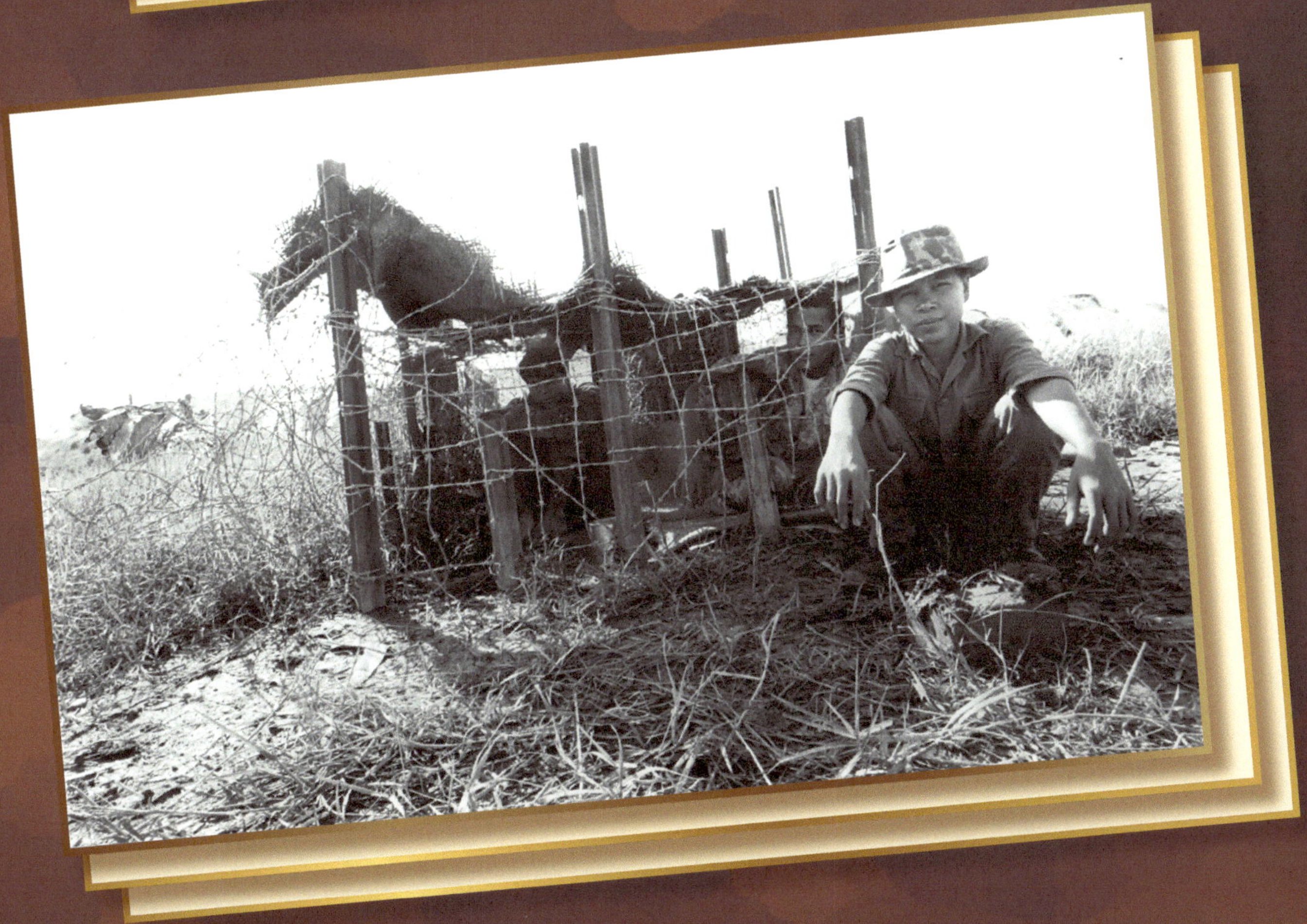

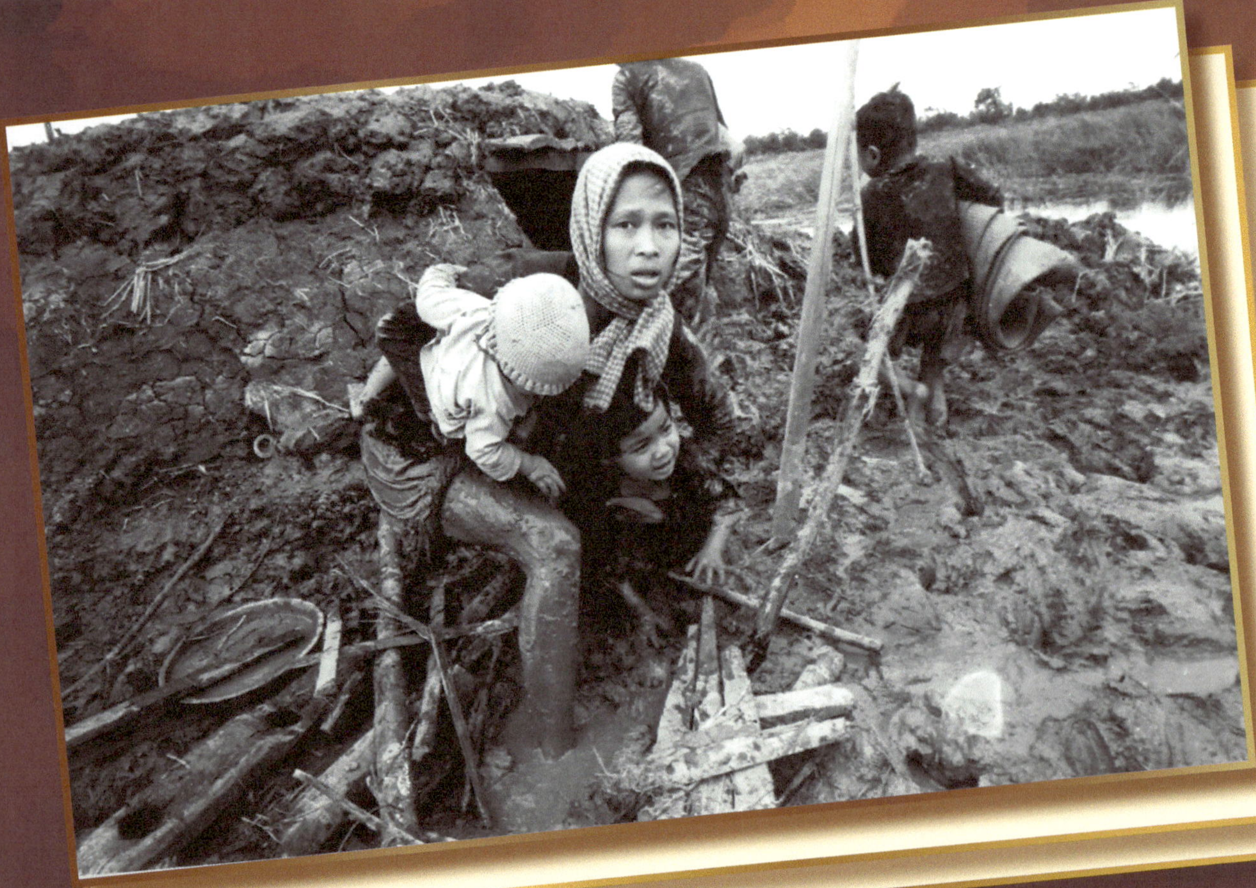

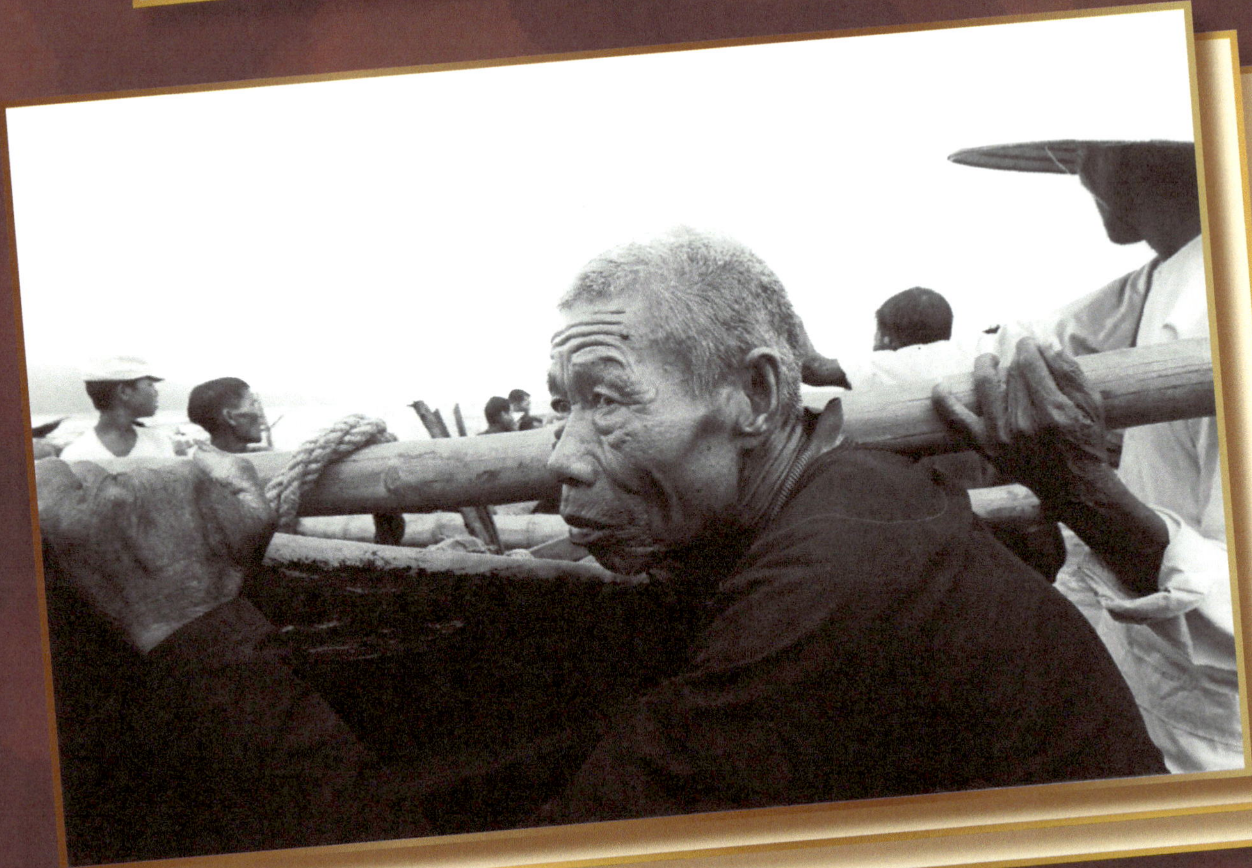

on Dana and Sean's behalf. I also contacted any people I knew, or friends knew on the New Left in the US; people who had been to Hanoi, friends of Sihanouk. I feel that these people are more important in the eyes of Hanoi and Sihanouk than any US Govt. spokesman. Recently I visited the North Vietnamese in Laos, I asked them for any information they might have and I applied for a visa to Hanoi in order to see the Sihanouk Representative there. I am pretty sure I will not get a visa, but they might appreciate my application as an act of faith in their govt. I also went to India while Mme. Binh, Head of the NLF, was making a state visit there, but I did not get to see her. I have written Dana and Sean letters; they probably wont be delivered, but it was worth a try. In all my dealings with the North Vietnamese, the NLF and Sihanouk, I have always stressed Dana and Sean's objection to US involvment in Indo-China, their position as non-combattants and their anti-war sentiments. If I do not get any word soon, I will go to Paris to see the Pro-Sihanouk people there.

Many people have been very kind in helping me contact the right people on the New Left. If you have any friends who are communists, or know people who might have influence with Hanoi or Sihanouk, you might contact them and have them write a letter to the proper people. Make sure you stress Sean's pacificism, and the fact that he was captured by Pro-Sihanouk Cambodians, NOT the North Vietnamese or NLF. Recently, a friend of Sean's, a cameraman for CBS, went to Cuba. While he is there he is going to see Castro concerning Sean's capture, since it is well known that Castro was a great admirer of Sean's father. I feel that any personal contacts like this are helpful.

I am sorry I did not write to you sooner; I felt that Time Magazine was taking care to send you any information they might have, but recently I found out this may not be true. I have just packed all of Sean's belongings for safe keeping. I will keep them here in Saigon as long as I stay here, and when I leave I will have them sent to you, or anywhere you suggest. Enclosed is an inventory; TIME has a copy and I have a copy. There is not much of value, but a lot of things that meant a great deal to Sean. All of the film he took is stored in an air conditioned room, and should be alright. The film is the most important thing, he has taken many good pictures and they should be preserved.

If you wish to get hold of me, you can do so through CBS News, since Dana was working for them. Please use the address below, which is much quicker than sending mail through the South Vietnamese mail. For very quick contact, call CBS New York, ask for Mr. Robert Little, and he can telex me immediately in Saigon. I will keep you informed if I receive any information. Please send me your telephone number. I am sending a copy of this letter to Dr. Joseph Doane in West Palm Beach to forward to you in case you are not in Iowa. If there is anything I can do for you, let me know. I know it is useless to say "Don't worry," everyone says that to me and I doesnt do much good, but I have faith that Dana and Sean are alive, and I expect them home any day. I mean this.

              Sincerely
              Louise Stone
              Louise Stone
              CBS News
              JUSPAO Press Mission
              APO San Francisco 96243

SEAN FLYNN
6, RUE NICOLAS CHUQUET
PARIS XVII⁵

Dear Lih —

5/31/65

First you are sweet to have sent me a check which as an incipient philanthopist I will immediately donate to S.O.U.S.E. (Save Our Underprivileged SEAN from Erosion). Secondly I found out about Mother's Day from a girl who is, but isn't if you know what I mean (Not guilty, moi). but the thought is there so ~~Happy~~ Mummy's day.

To answer your rather complicated question as to why I live here and not in the U.S. where the bread is (I agree there is more, even in T.V.) I was playing a game with two other friends & Cooky called STOP. On a piece of paper there are seven ~~Headings~~ such as Musciens, authors, Cities, actors, battlefields, painters the object being to complete a name from a given letter before the others. for example, the letter M one would put Menuin, the violinist for muscien; Mauriac for author, Montpellier for city etc. — I didn't do as well as the others in such esoteric subjects as music, opera, painters etc. because I was never exposed to this culture of Europe not found in America. What I'm trying to say is that I'm learning here what I never could there. I have an idea: Why don't you think about buying a little house in the country ~~is~~ here and fixing it up, or a little villa on the riviera — for a hobby, of course. love

Sean

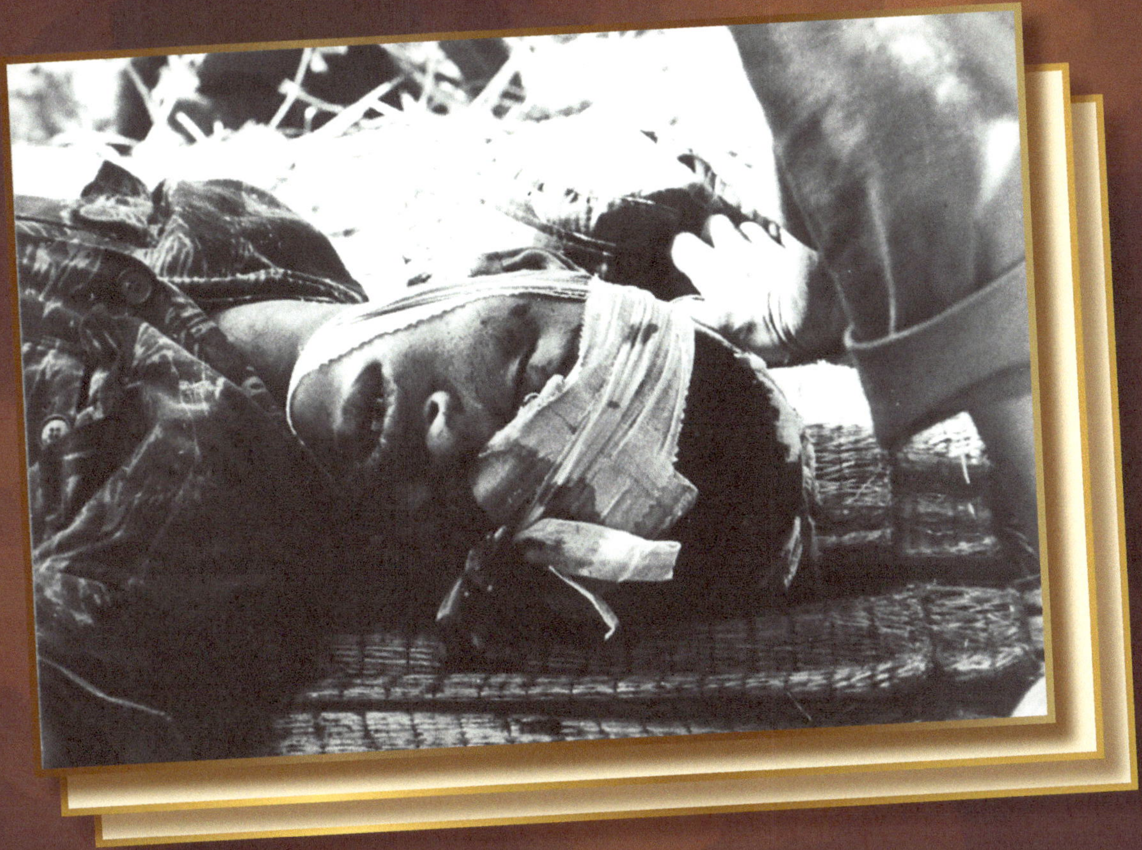

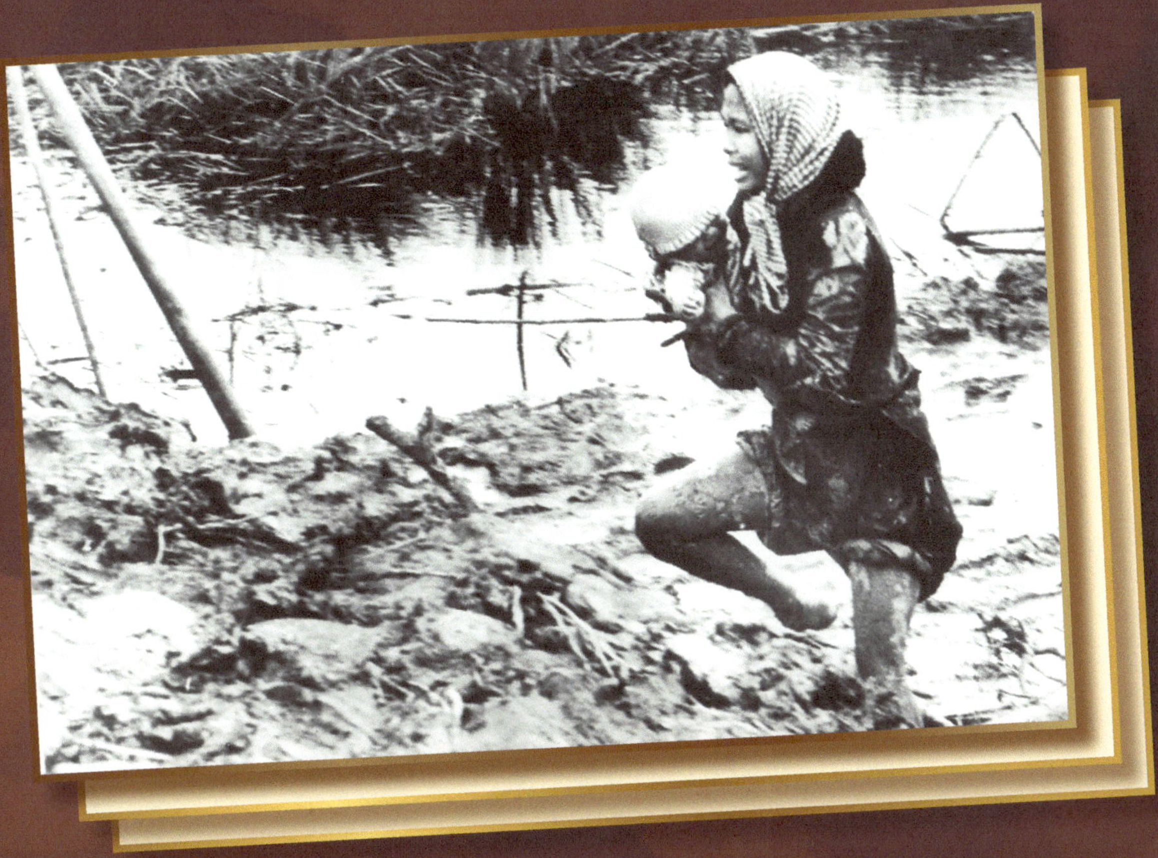

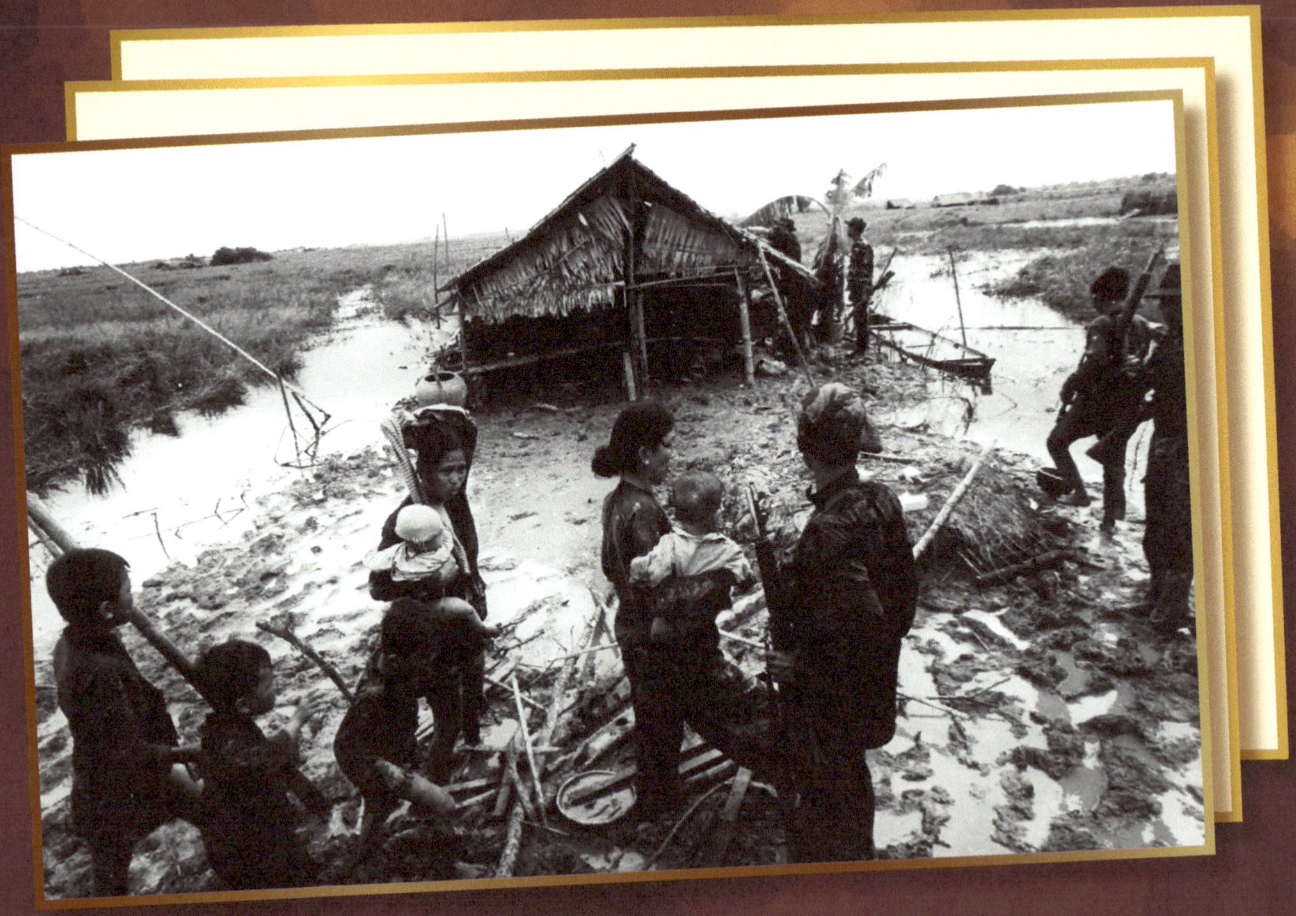

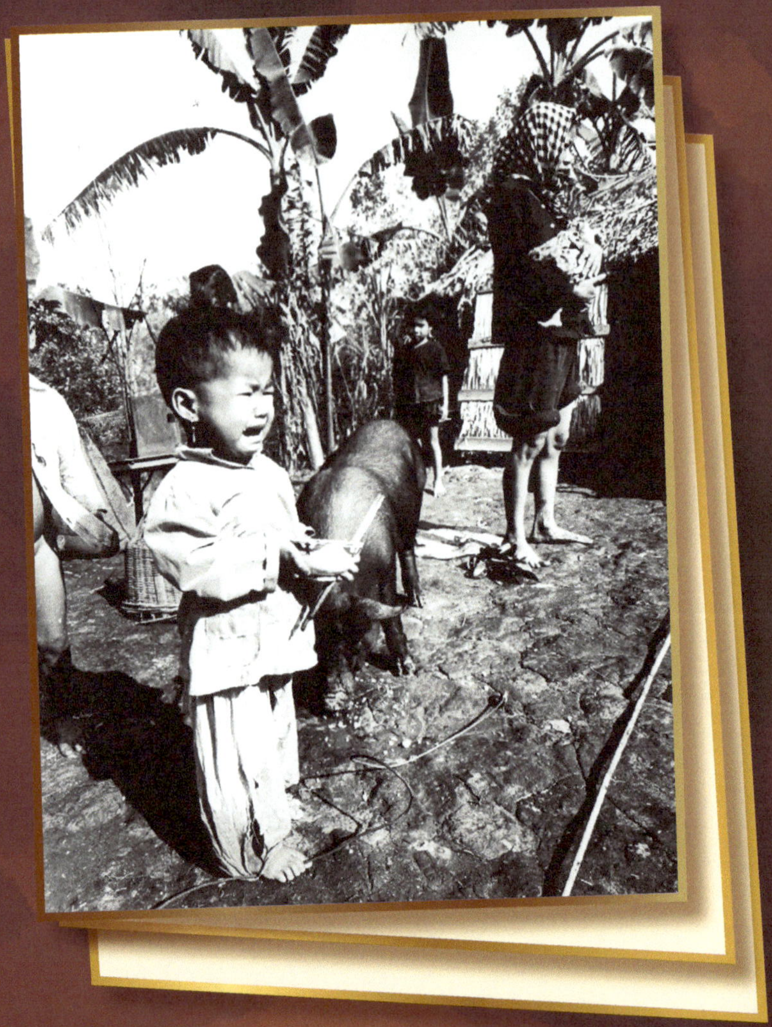

3. Please show this letter to Steve Cutter & tell him to come on over here →

Jan. 29, 1964
Paris

Dear Parent —

Where am I? Where was I? What have I done? Why didn't I write? Where will I go? etc. All questions which must be in your mind and which, because of their nature & complication, will be difficult to answer, but I'll try.

First I'm now in Paris having just returned from the Swamplands (the Sunderbans) of South East Pakistan or more simply, East Bengal. I spent 4 weeks on a little houseboat, never seeing a white man speaking only a little Bengali and working for the Forest Dept. hunting tiger.

This rather odd occupation was offered me because 1) there were several man-eating tigers running loose and nobody to really get in and kill them 2) I asked to go.

My little houseboat covered about 20 miles a day, propelled by currents & oars — I finally got my tiger and the offer of a permanent job with the gov't as white hunter, also a bounty.

I might add that I gained a good bit of experience and story material (I was also working for a quarterly magazine in

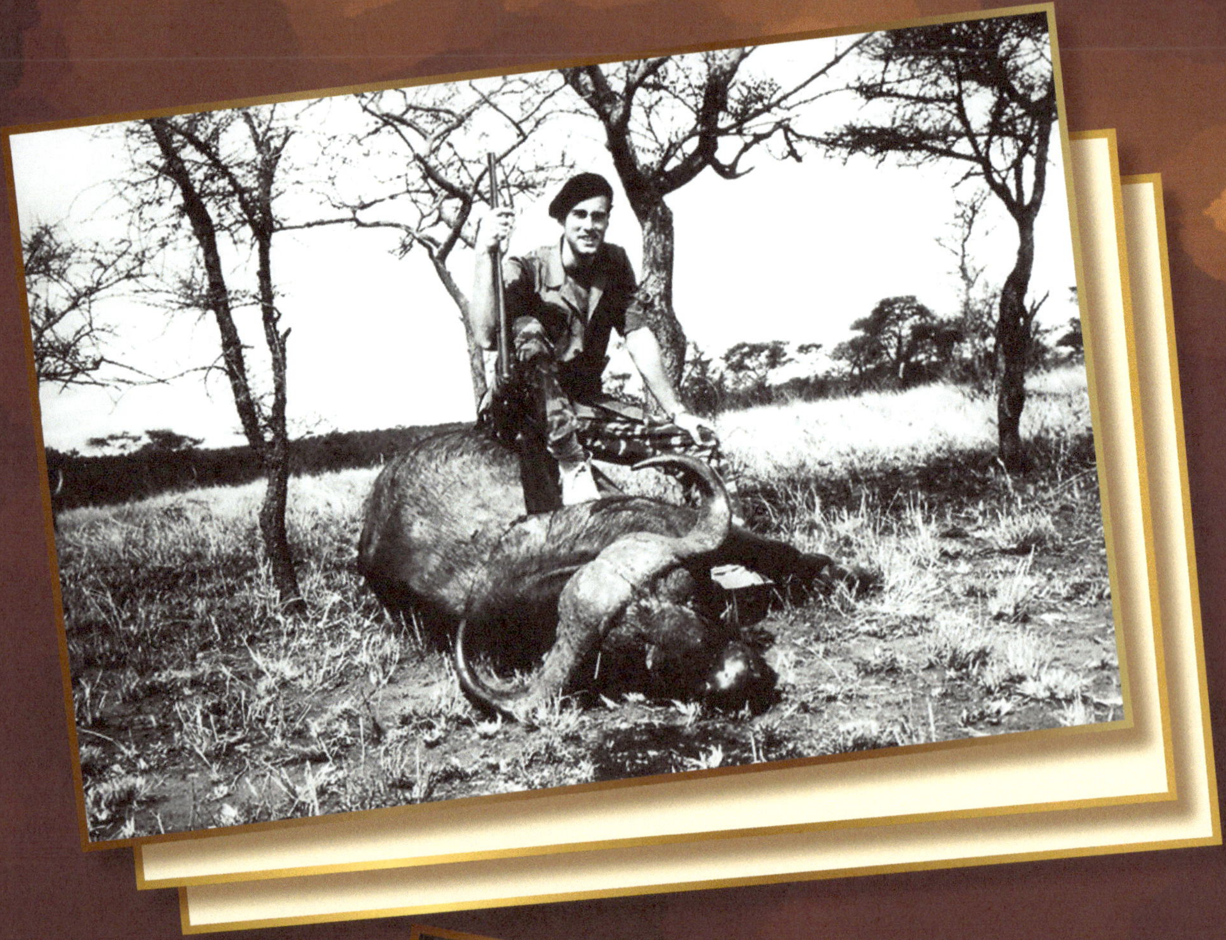

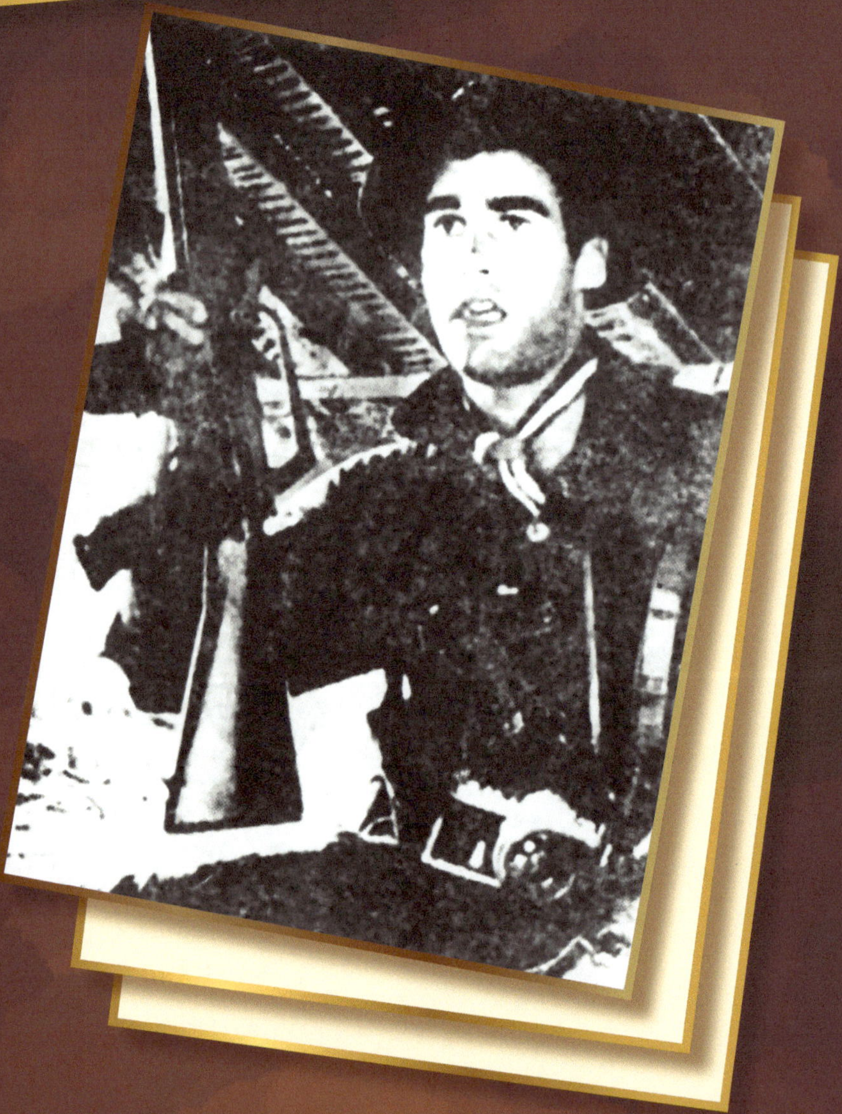

②
West Pakistan)

One day a boatload of natives searched me out (I was poaching deer with a Forest Guard, our only means of fresh meat) - they told me a man had been killed - they took me to the spot and I tracked the poor fellow down by following a blood spoor. I sat up in a nearby tree over the body but the 'Manus-Kai' (man-eater) never came back. As you can imagine, this letter doesn't do justice to my experiences - 6 fantastic weeks where a man is valued by his beard and what he can do with his hands & brain - quite a switch from this film 'merde' - I spent holidays with some friends in Karachi where I made plans to go next summer to hunt 'Marco Polo' sheep, the rarest & largest in the world, found only in the northern passes of Hunza & Gilgit - Shangri-la - the roof of the world.

So please accept this belated Christmas greeting although you're probably sick of the word - I couldn't have written from where I was - news of a man's death took 3 days to reach the nearest forest station. Emergency Please send ½ dozen tubes of Crest Toothpaste - Paris
  All my love Jean

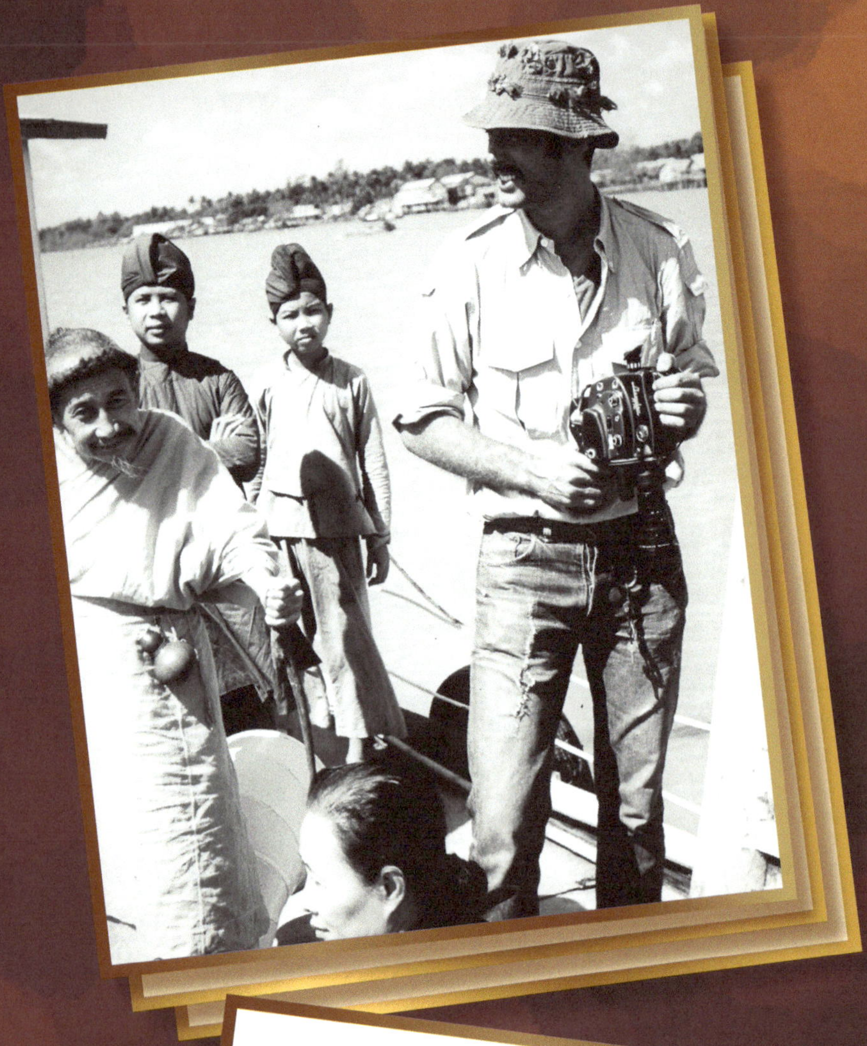

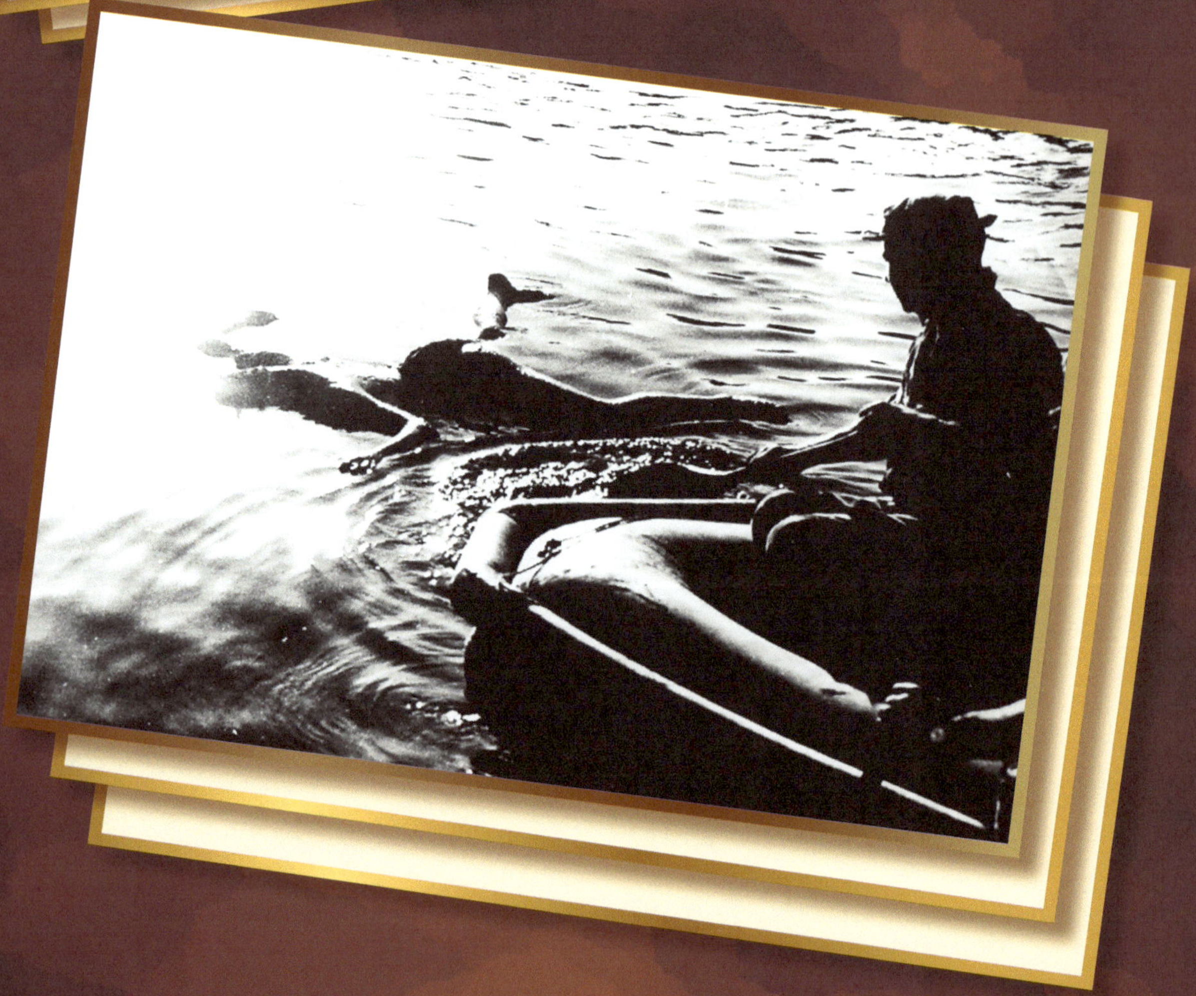

COMPAGNIA CINEMATOGRAFICA MONDIALE
ROMA - Via G. A. Guatiani, 14 - Tel. 863.748

Berlin 3/8/63

Dear Mom —

Well it's finally started and I can only let out a sigh of relief! Fortunately I was wrong about the director who is actually a very nice fellow of no mean talent. The script is being rewritten every day — my conclusion! that the picture won't make a penny but that it is more valuable than if I had made a big-box office smash in another swashbuckler. I really needed a modern film — and judging from some of the rushes, this will give me a big boost.

Berlin is a rather funny place — everybody lives like there's no tomorrow (they're probably right), consequently they're not as "sour" as the rest of the Germans. The other night I was reading in bed — all was very quiet. Suddenly I heard machine guns shooting at some poor bastard who was trying to escape (I live in Spandau, quite close to the border). It makes one realize not only how lucky one is but also it points out a terrible debasement of human dignity — nobody should be shot because he wants to cross a border. It's like being surprised in the bathroom with your pants down — got to go   love Sean
P.S. Orson wouldn't make it (no surprise) but Ferrer's ok

THE NORFOLK HOTEL
PROPRIETORS: BLOCK HOTELS LTD.
P.O. BOX 64
NAIROBI - KENYA
TELEPHONE: 27431

28/3/65

Dear Mother —

I believe the last time I wrote you was from Nairobi — Not much time has past since then but many circumstances and much distance, has.

I returned to Ceruska and spent a week gathering supplies, licences and equipment together for my safari. By this time I know quite a few people (as you soon do here - not in a busybody way but in a more or less pioneer atmosphere one makes aquantances easier than in civilization) I borrowed a tent here, a bed there, and "taka-taka" ("everything" in Swahili). I had one good gunbearer lined up but he was a poacher and

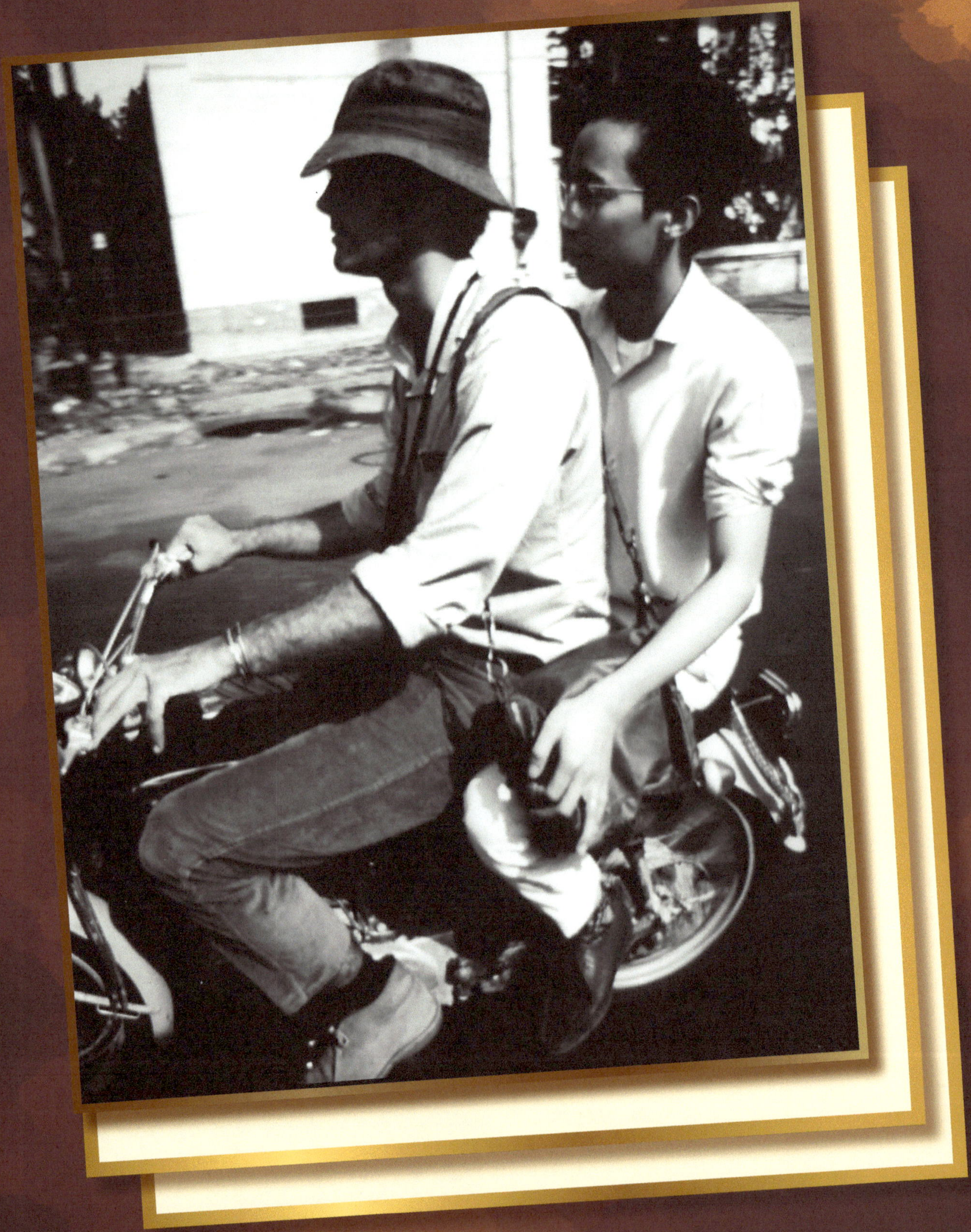

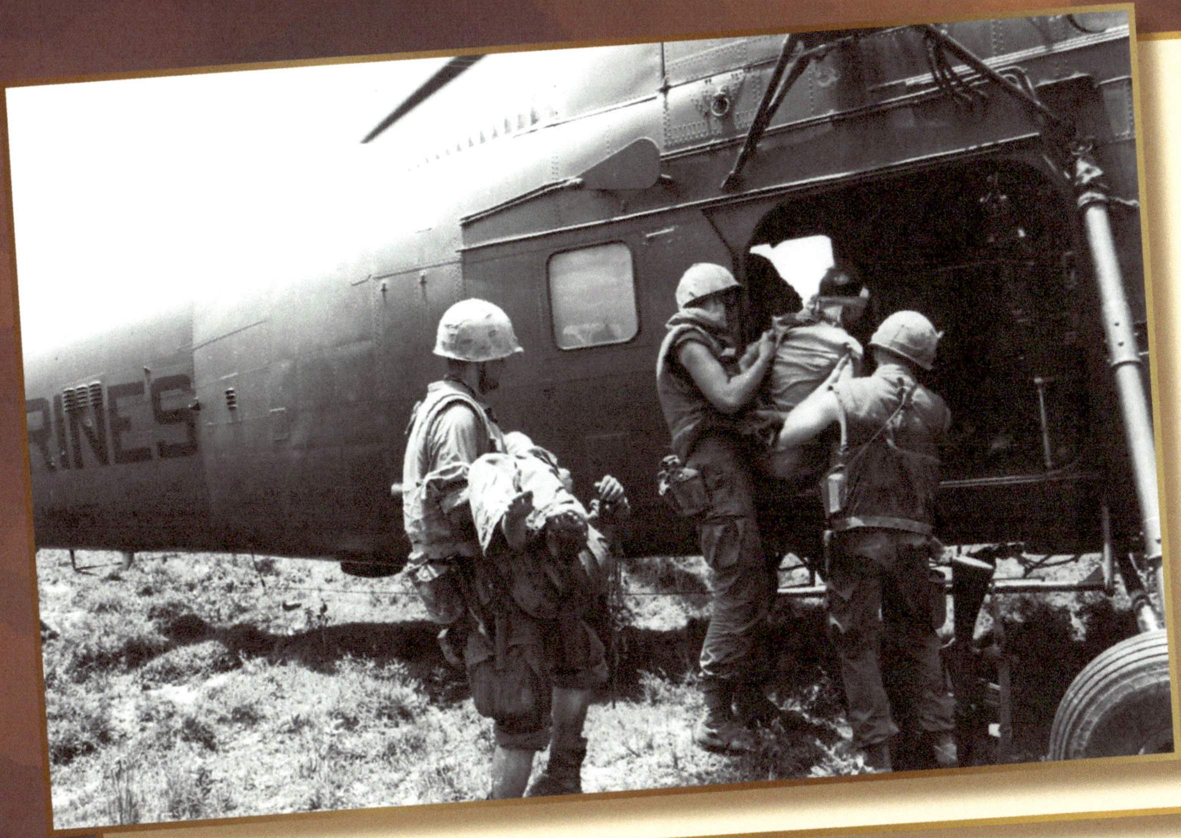
RINES

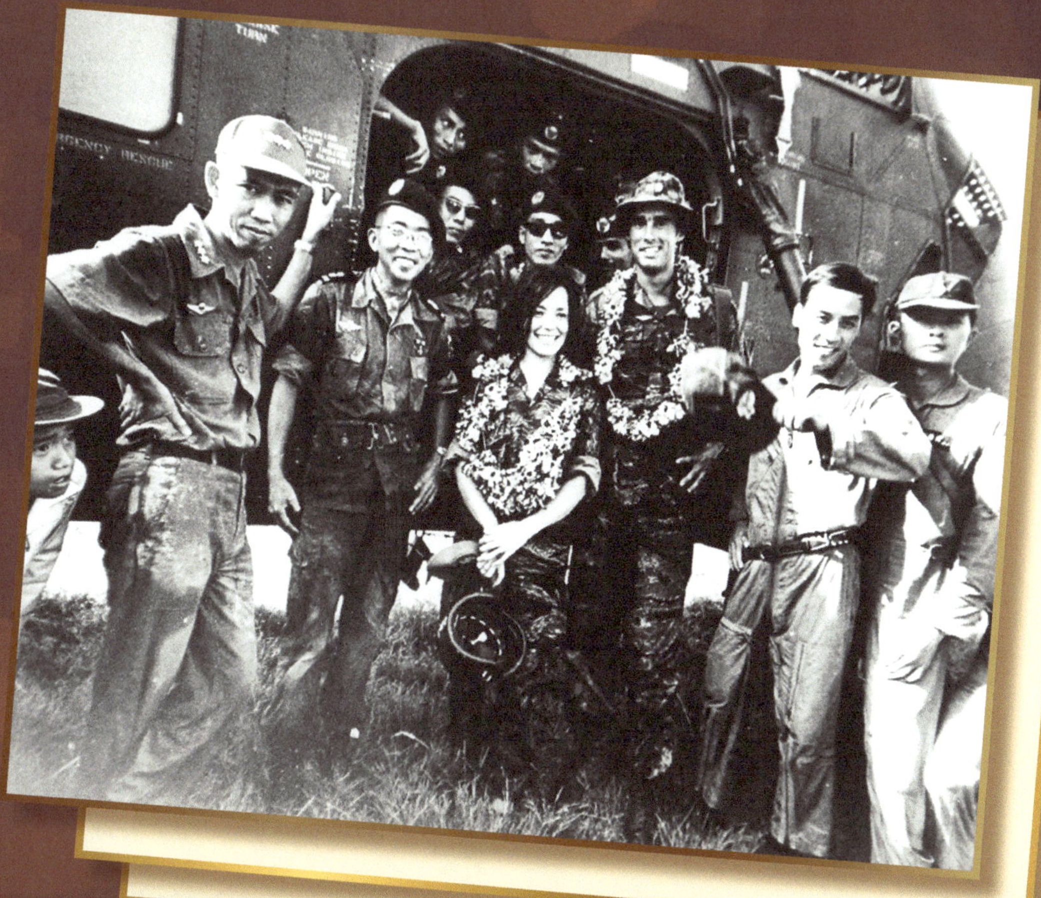

was disillusioned when I wouldn't let him bring his bow & arrow in the car. Actually I got two good chaps, the other a cook called MZÉE ("old man") who bakes the best fresh bread I've ever eaten.

We're now in Northern Masailand about 200 miles south of Arusha. There are many elephants here but I'm not shooting until I get a big one — over 80 lbs I hope. Naturally we have to look over a lot but my tracking is getting pretty good now and when the trail splits, my gunbearer and I do too.

Since it's so dry we had to camp near a permanent water hole with the Masai and all their bloody cows — there are millions of flys too and I'd send you the one walking down my pen but they might put a surcharge on the letter.

It's difficult to describe camp, very simple with no luxuries but you'd be surprised how much you can put in a Short Wheelbase Land-Rover along with ~~three~~ men. I think the best part is the wonderful nights — moonfilled, temperate and filled with African sounds — Hyena almost came in my tent last night to steal a hock of Impala. Food good but want to try broiling the end of an elephant trunk — recipe: dig hole, line with stones, light fire, when stones hot put in trunk and cover with more hot rocks — leave 3 days and meat slips out of skin. Sound good?   love Sean

Saigon 19/5/66

Just returned from three weeks in Malaysian Borneo

I have had my hands full here with an ambush at night where the men on the right and in front of me were wounded. Perhaps you saw my photo of the Viet Cong tortured in TIME magazine. The Americans are very unhappy about that one! Borneo was a nice change and very profitable at $100 day plus expenses. I wanted to see the guerilla war there with the British vs. the Indonesians — went by canoe 160 kil. up the large Rajang River and spent a few days in a native longhouse — the men covered with tatoos + bones in the ears + bare breasted native women etc.

March 5 1968 — 0845 —
KHE SAAN, Vietnam

I finally made it here after trying for three days in Danang. There is a press center here with air conditioned rooms, a bar and warm food. I went to town with the younger brother of a friend I knew a year ago who knows Tim Page. We found a young girl who's brother had a cyclo — and wanted to take us to an opium den... but since we were coming to Khe Sahn in the morning we said no. It is dangerous flying in here. The Viets are all around this marine base. 4 square miles of armed camp and 5000 marines. Around there are 30 to 40,000 Viet-minh and we can see their trenchs that come within 75 meters of our barbed wire perimeter. I am living with the sea-bees, the Navy construction men. They have the best bunkers that will withstand everything but a direct hit from a 122 mm chineese rocket. The rockets fall sporadically and I wear helmet and armoured vest which we never did a year ago. The war is very different here now. The Viet minh (now called NVA) have artillery, tanks and a lot of supplies. When the crachin lift the planes napalm around our perimeter and we see them digging. When our plane landed yesterday we were hit by DCA.

I am supposed to go to Thailand next week for the London Sunday Times. We are going to do the U.S. troop buildup in Bankok. Then to Laos for the opium pictures. I'll return in 3 weeks. I am sharing an appartment on the rue Catinat

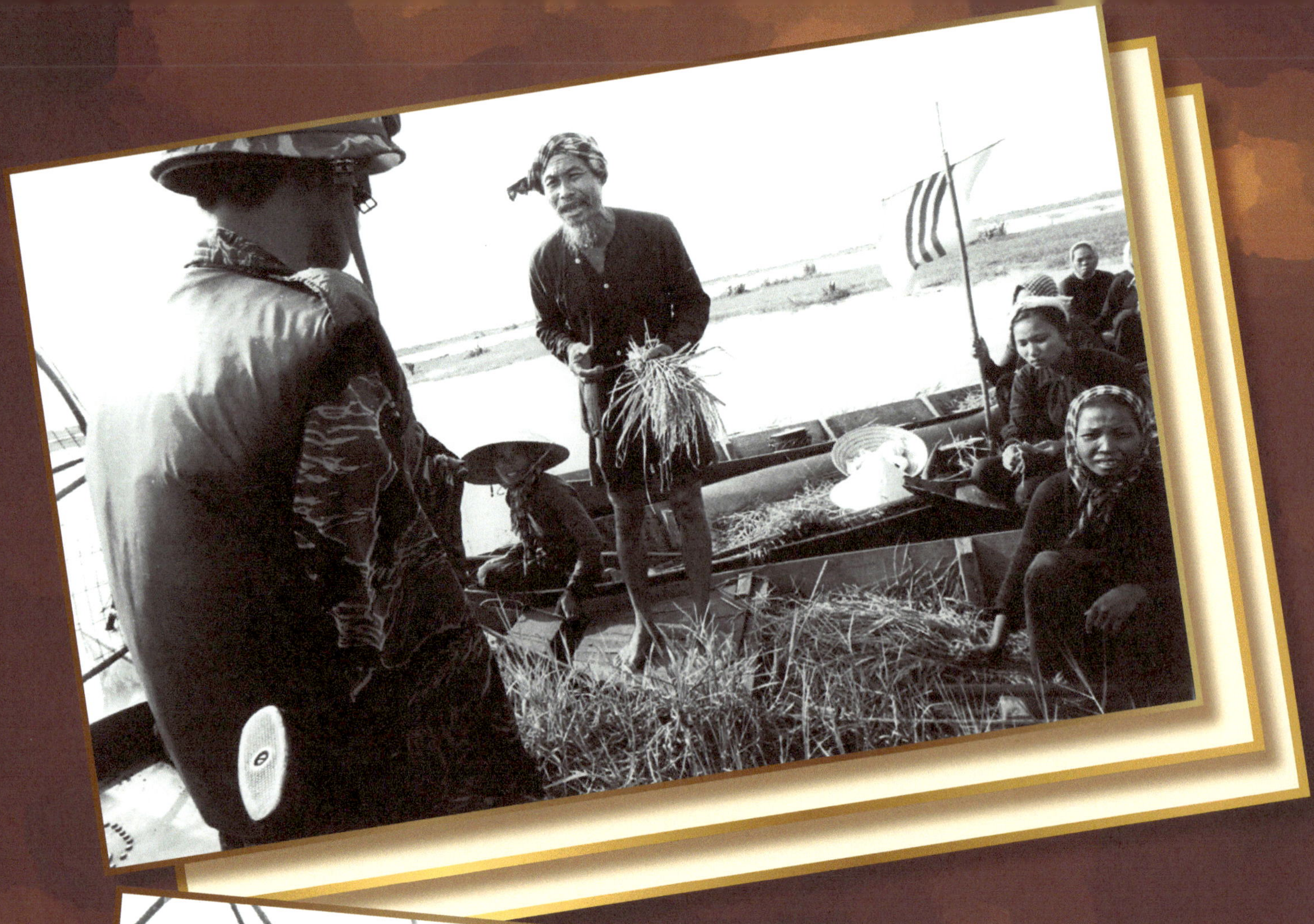

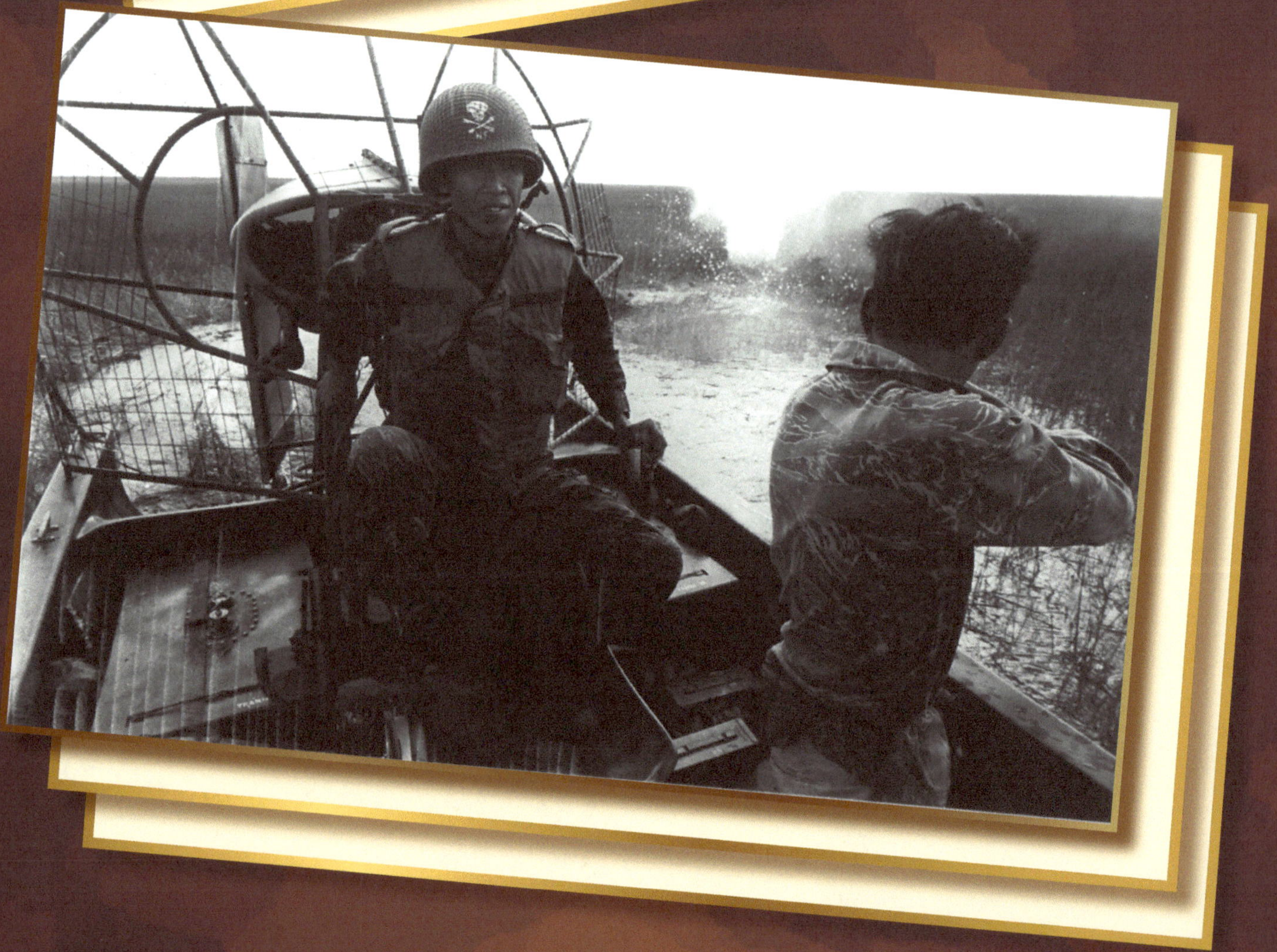

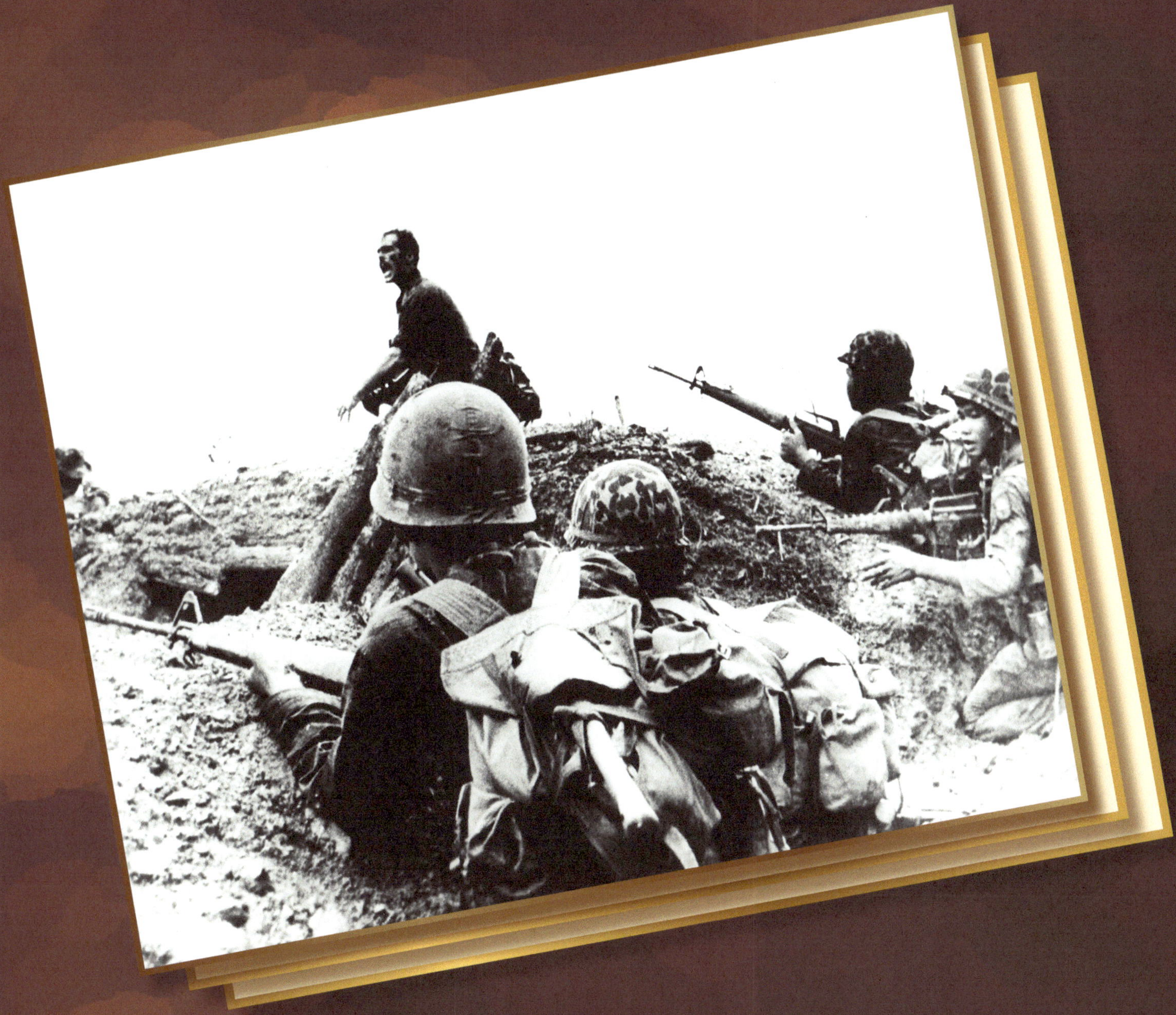

June 8 1968
Saigon

My mail comes late now because I stay in Danang. I have an old friend and his wife who have rented a house there. He is a photographer also and we have gone to the field together — his name is Dana Stone and he is good. The most fighting is North in I corps. Near Khe Sahn, the DMZ, Dong Ha etc. Always the Marines. I was offered a staff job with CBS-TV as a cameraman. I worked very hard and got better film than the staff people of NBC so they offered about 450$ a week. As you know me, I turned it down. I make much less but I can go and do what I want. Which reminds me! You didn't say if you had received the film I sent from here. It's very important. I don't want to think of filming this action and having the film lost. The way things look I'll probably stay here for some time.

Many journalists are leaving Saigon as if the war was over but the fighting at the DMZ is more fierce than ever. Rats are leaving a sinking ship it seems. At least war news and pictures are less + less important.

Danang
May 19

Spent a month at Kontum with a long range patrol — four men (including me) dropped by helicopter in the middle of the jungle and for 4 days spy on the NVA. Very exciting; especially when we are walking down one trail and they come in the opposite direction. Fast shooting over in ten seconds. Only happened once though.

I'm off in fifteen minutes to go with the Marines on a new operation so I'll write fast and maybe in the field if I have time.

②

June 8, 1968
Saigon

I feel that I'll stay a long while in Asia. The war very possibly will be negotiated in the next six months and I certainly don't want to leave before then. I'm doing the best work I ever have.

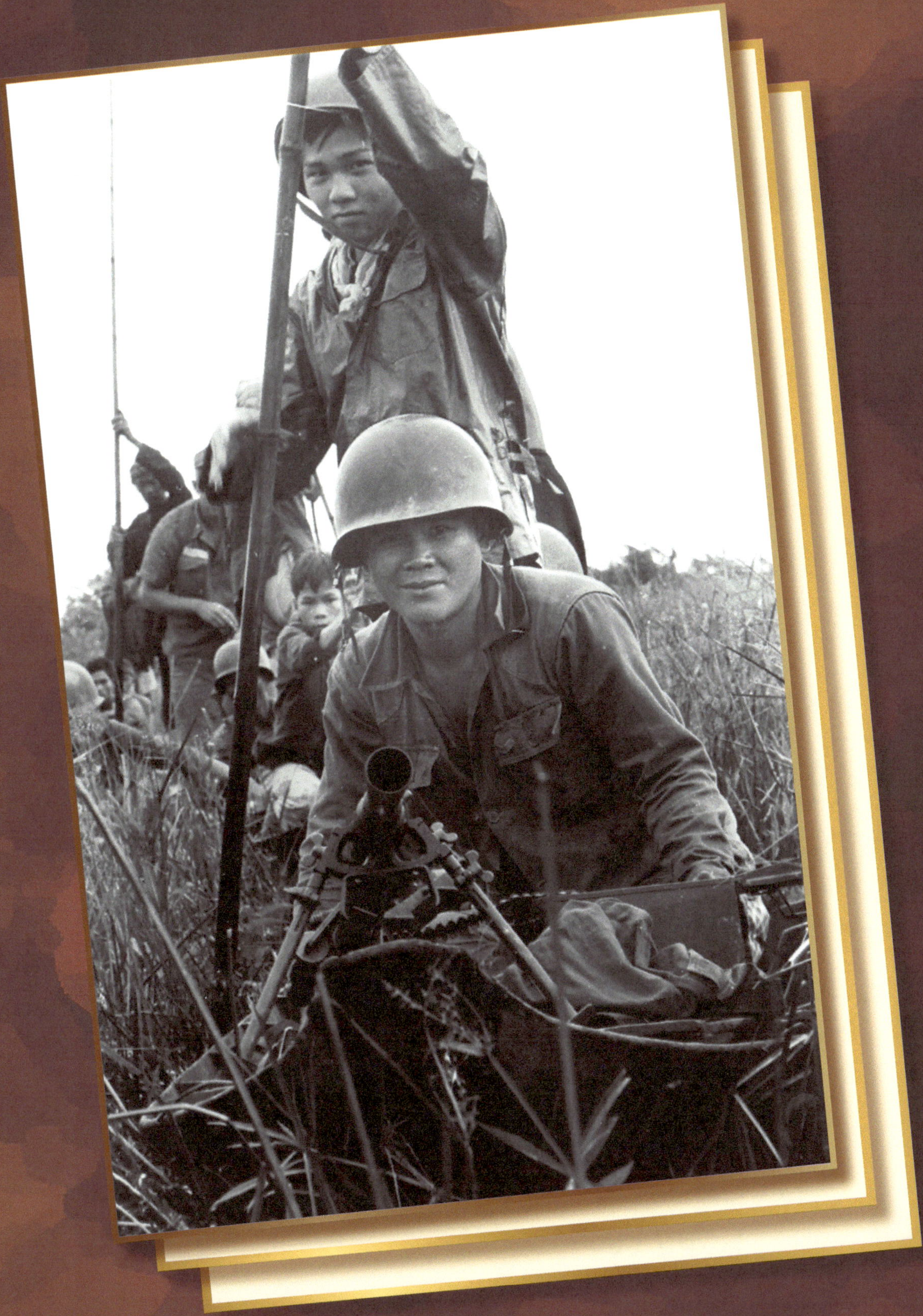

DJAKARTA (1969)
Nov.
Saturday

Dear Ol' friends
The Gods must have blessed your missive — might even have set a record of sorts by getting thru two notoriously bad mail services. — How to start?

I'm now on bail here in DJAKARTA pending trial (God knows when) for assault & battery (number 351 Indonesian statute) destruction of property etc. Swanson might have told you I was hung on a chick — true! name of Jaesmi (pronounced Jax-s-mi). One day my lovely brown and myself hired a taxi to go mountainwards — driver — a pimp remembers her house — advance 2 weeks — tells Jax's servant she to be ready at 2 PM in her best dress to go and fuck a rich chinaman. Wow did I blow! $45 I arrive with club — 14:00 arrive pimp, 3 others in view Mercedes Benz — Well now flying wigged he did. He strides out uh driveway & wails over mere, windows, windshield headlight grill shattering cracking 'accidente' — rich chinaman goes from hard on to horror in 1/5 second — people fleeing — I catch pimp and blow him away — later — me to jail for 3 days — now got a lawyer.

I had planned return for Swanson wedding but now fuck all knows. Anyway I want to split with my chick (she's still in 11th grade so must wait end school term this month) so I may abduct this witch or spend 3 to 5 in kebayoran dal. I'm glad Dana in house (at least till I return and find out how much he's lifted)

Thanks for sounds, needed same as passport $500 stolen with them. Too bad about Bali but maybe not — you wouldn't have returned. I hope to buy land/hootch there.

INEFFABALY
S

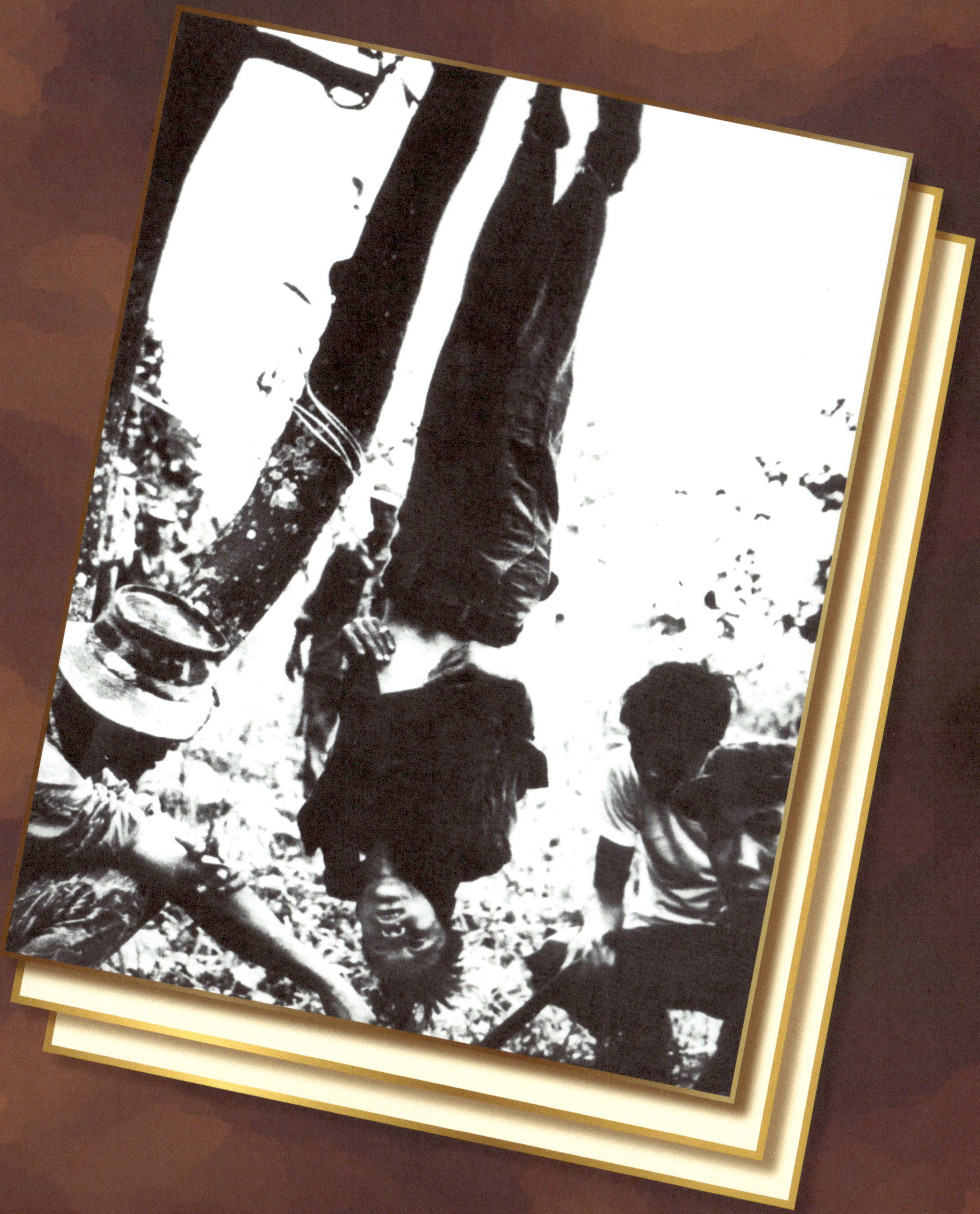

Wounded — Sean Flynn, working as a cameraman for the Columbia Broadcasting System, was wounded slightly by grenade fragments during a counterattack by U.S. Special Forces on an enemy squad 85 miles south of Da Nang, South Vietnam. Flynn, 27, son of the late actor Errol Flynn, was hit in the chest but did not require hospital care.

The Des Moines Register

Sept. 2nd, 1968 "Des Moines Register"

August 11

Nobody brought my mail for three weeks to Danang so I didn't know what is happening in the world. I rushed this film.

The war is 'over' as far as large scale fighting is concerned. I went on Marine operations to area's that before were full of NVA – nothing! I believe the politicians made a secret deal in Paris.

I am going this week to Kathmandu. My friend and several others have mixed in politics here by supporting an old ascetic bonze, the Dao Dua, or 'coconut monk'. I could write a mile and will except that I have little energy & must say much. I've documented our involvement on film. The press has taken notice. Now John & myself will go soon with the NLF to do another film project. Only you know there. We will probably be kicked out on our return by the government. It will be dangerous as the Americans will bomb us.

Until this project I will be unable to judge how I feel physically. However, I am convinced the future for me will be to live simply in a country like Laos or Cambodia.

Dear Lil — August 25 Sài-gòn

Sorry about letter writing – no excuse even though the Press mission was moved after a large fire. Reminded of Yossarian in the book *Catch-22* who finds it difficult to write home so advises everybody that he is going on a dangerous mission and will be unable to write until his return. It is difficult to explain what happens here – to explain would confuse and make you nervous and it would seem more dangerous than it is. Frankly my biggest problem is that it is too calm although the VC have attacked Tay Ninh, Danang, and other cities in an apparent bid to bolster their bargaining position in Paris during the convention.

I'll probably remain here for several more months. My film is being shipped regularly to Paris. It will be very different I promise you – bloody, funny, beautiful, controversial. Read August Esquire – Michael Herr article called *Hell Sucks* (terrible title, not his) but good writing and explains it from Marines point of view. We spent several months together in Danang – a good friend.

Luv, S

Sept. 17, 1965

You may have heard that I was wounded! This is true, however it was slight. I believe I finally got what I want here. I have seen the color slides from the action and they are the most important. I went to a Special Forces Camp that was surrounded by North Vietnamese. In a three day battle the Chinese Nungs assaulted a hill near the camp held by the enemy. It was raining — they threw hand grenades down on us. I was filming and the man ahead of me was killed. We finally reached the summit and in bitter hand to hand fighting seized the outpost. At the end the place was littered with bodies and material, muddy and we were exhausted. Montagnard women from a nearby village wandered around digging their husbands who had been shot out of the collapsed bunkers. I also have a tape (my recorder was on) so I have gotten what I went most, the best story of an assault ever filmed. I now have to do the pick up shots — marching, eating, landscapes.

I dig danang very much as I believe I told you. It is a bit lonesome but I bought a Honda and have driven nearly to Hue thru small Vietnamese fishing villages that are free from Americans.

There are good restaurants, provinces that cook excellent frogs legs & crabs — also a beautiful beach with hold on — surf boards from California. Good surf too. I have done a lot of good thinking and will miss it but soon I must return to work on the film.

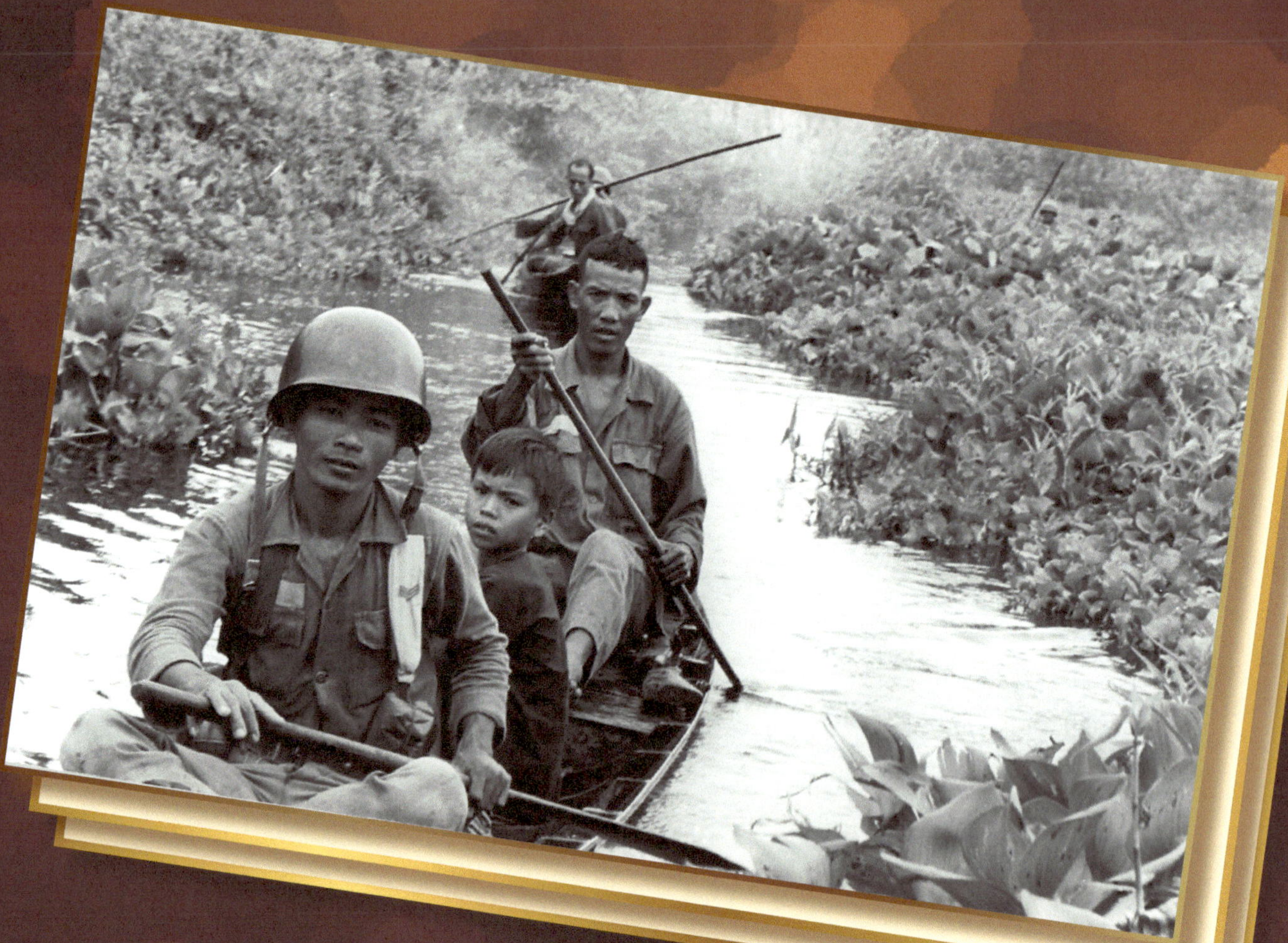

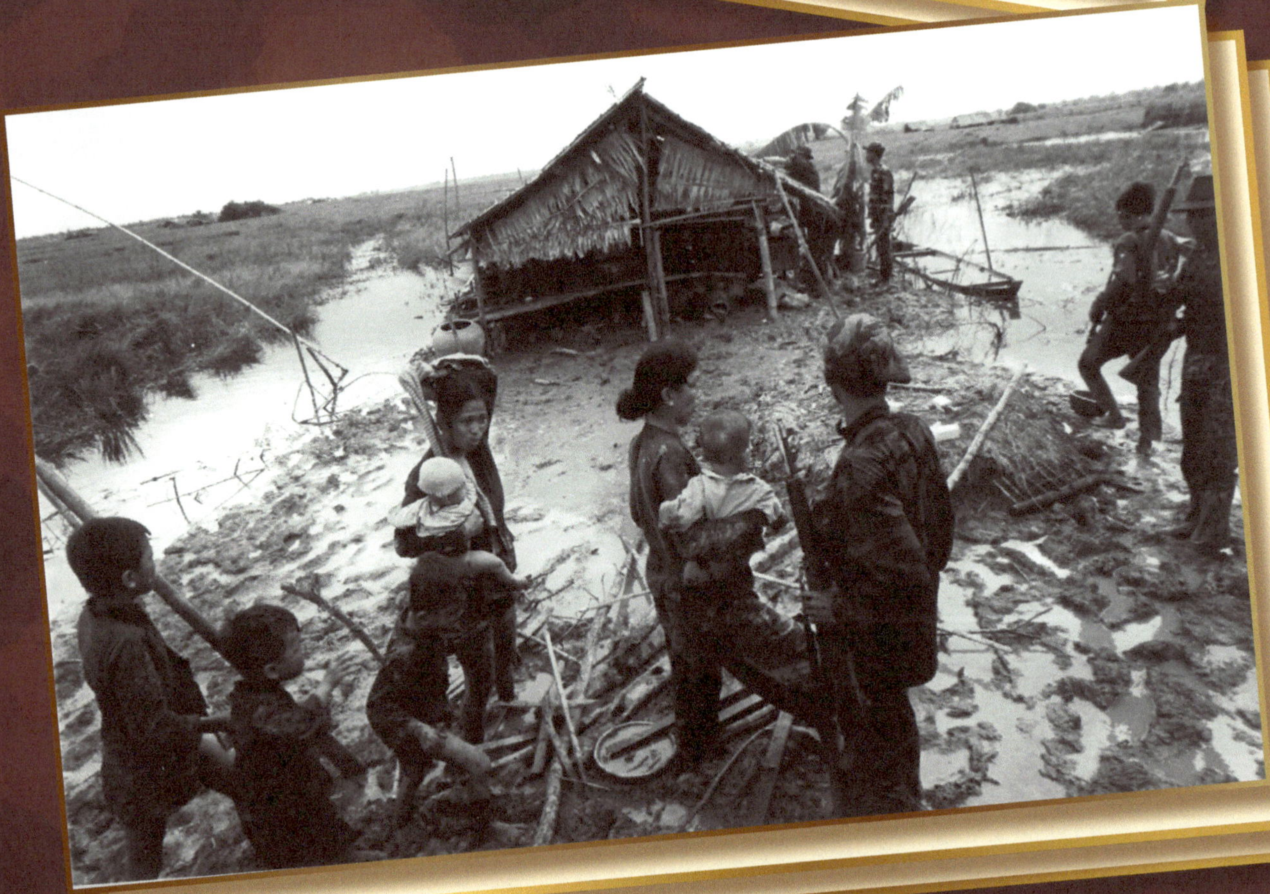

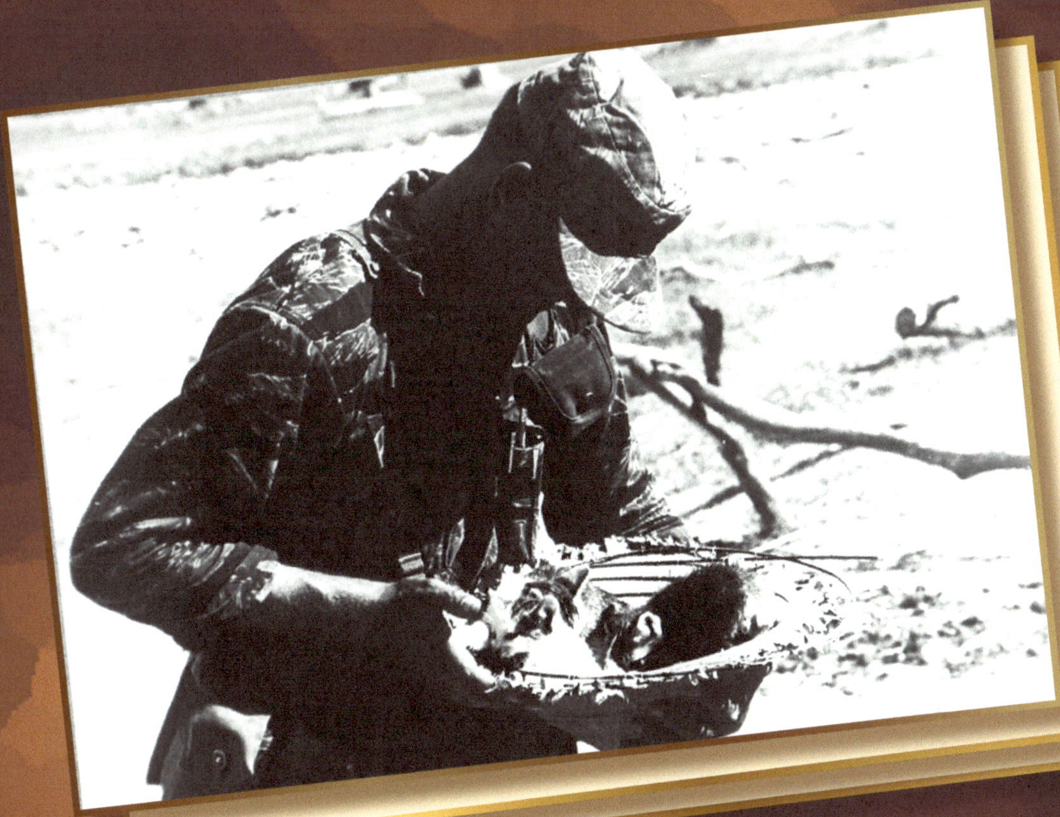

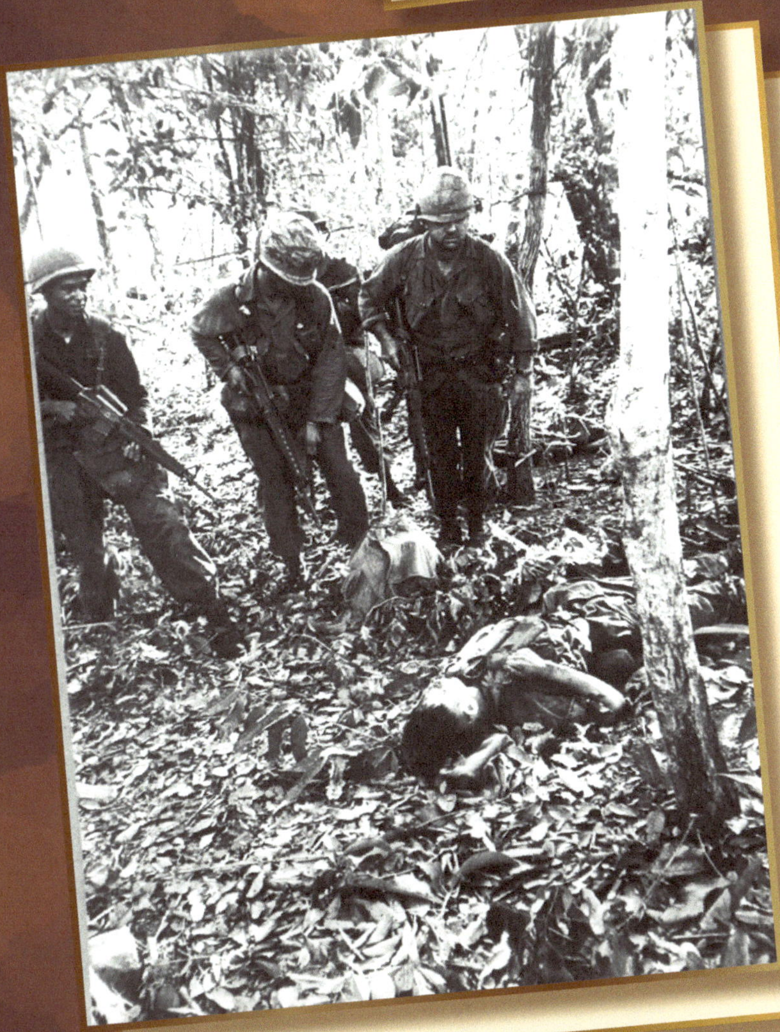

Sept 19, 1968
Saigon

Dear Mom—

Everything okay here as I said in telegram—all arm, legs, eyes etc. intact which is more than I can say for the poor bastard in front of me. I received two of your letters, the second obviously after the mishap. You asked for further information. We assaulted a hill with Special Forces mercenaries held by NVA. We finally took the hill after a bitter fight — I was fortunate to have made what I feel (and others among Life, AP etc photographers) are the best combat photos (in color) ever made. Although they are difficult to unload (due as you pointed out, to lack of interest in Viet things) they will form the backbone of a book I hope to be able to flog. A good friend in New York is working on this. So I may have to return to the U.S. around Christmastime. Coincidentally the film footage was pretty well filled by the same assault. It seems hard to believe but I'm getting near the end.

Now I need pick up shots — easy stuff like low altitude helicopter rides, G.I.'s eating in the field etc. Probably another two months will do it. I'd like to get down to visit Indonesia (where some old Viet friends from U.P.I. work) and Bali — Perhaps Nepal on the return to France. You must understand that I feel a bit vague after having experienced and photo-ed this assault and gotten away relatively unscathed.

Tim Page and John Steinbeck plan to visit the Dao Sect in the Delta — they control their own island complete with army etc. Very spiritual LSD type place to reflect for a few days, don't you think.

Was appalled at the Chicago scene — it confirms what I suspect — a very very large communication gap between two powerful groups. Civil war maybe? Wallace is a fascist, Nixon hasn't changed and Humphrey ~~probably honest~~ but incapable of leading U.S. ~~~~ anti war people

luv S—

I think I'll be sick with hepatitis soon. Little energy and me about to begin a great adventure.

                              Saturday
                              the 4 Jan.

My friend _____ and several others have mixed in politics here by supporting an old ascetic bonze, the Dao Dua, or 'coconut monk.' I could write a mile and will except that I have little energy & must say much. I've documented our involvement on film. The press has taken notice. Now John & myself will go soon with the NLF to do another film project. Only you know there. We will probably be kicked out on our return by the government. It will be dangerous as the Americans will bomb us.
  Until this project I will be unable to judge how I feel physically. However I am convinced the future for me will be to live simply in a country like Laos or Cambodia.

Goodwood PARK HOTEL SINGAPORE 9 · TELEPHONE 24141 · CABLE GOODWOOD

Nov 14, 1968

Dear Mother —
  I feel strange today as if touched by madness — don't be alarmed tho, its just a man of 28 yrs. (by Chinese count) taking stock on paper.
  I'm sorry that I fail to communicate. You see I've decided to stop or at least restrict things which I consider detrimental to frank understanding between people. No more platitudes, hypocrisy, injustice — a big order but as a wandering intellectual (I must consider myself that old school grades notwithstanding altho don't tell your friends & neighbors because they will say "if he's so smart what isn't he wealthy") well intellectual in the sense that I think more of socio-philosophical theoretics than day to day realistic pragmatism (ie a dreamer instead of a worker) but perhaps us grasshoppers are necessary.

Goodwood PARK HOTEL SINGAPORE 9 · TELEPHONE 24141 · CABLE GOODWOOD

I can feel a kinship with the hippies altho:
1) they bore me with their unrelenting hypothetical elysium and much as SDS bore me with their riots which are not my bag — No I have found my kind of violence in Vietnam and tho morally I condem the US involvement I do it knowing that personally I find an outlet and a need to have war around me and to see it and touch it when I want.
2) I'm too old believe it or not.
  So this letter is to inform you that I'm a hundred years old and if I don't write often its because I fail to be able to document and analyse (spelt wrong) my daily activities, hopes, fears, observations. Please bear with me.
  Tomorrow I'm going to Cambodia and find a little brown Cambodian girl and go sit in the ruins on Angkor (another dream?)
                    till later
                    luv (whatever that means)
                    S —

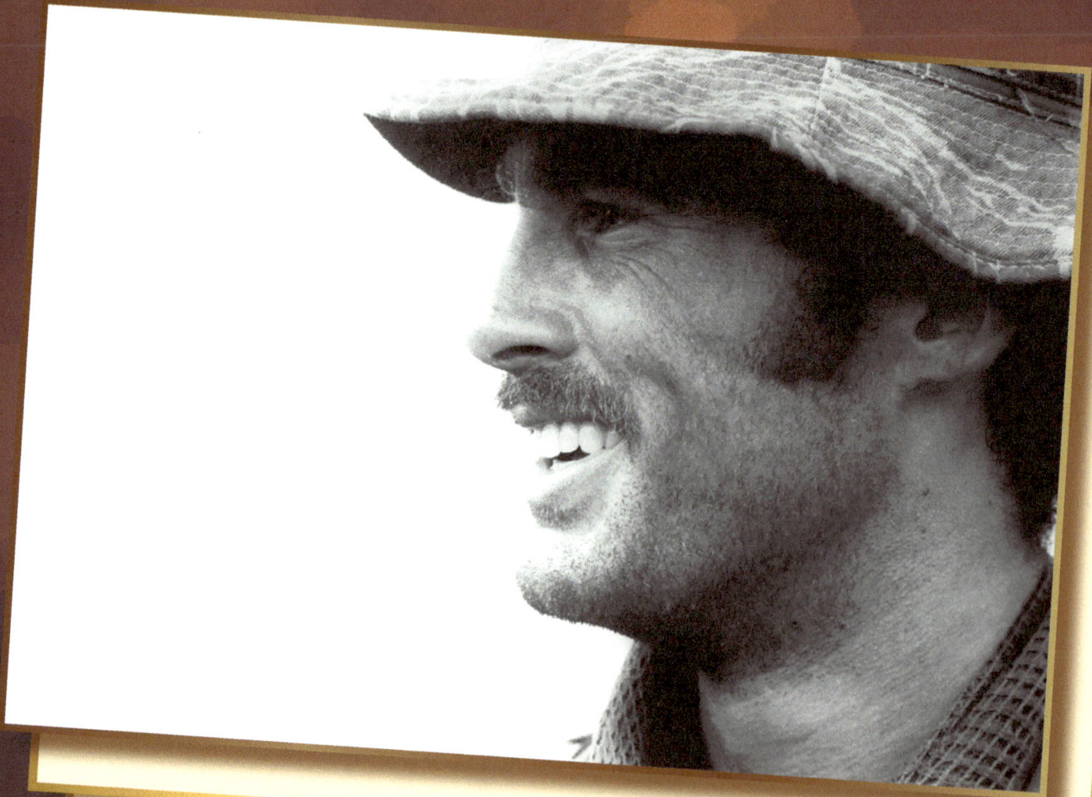

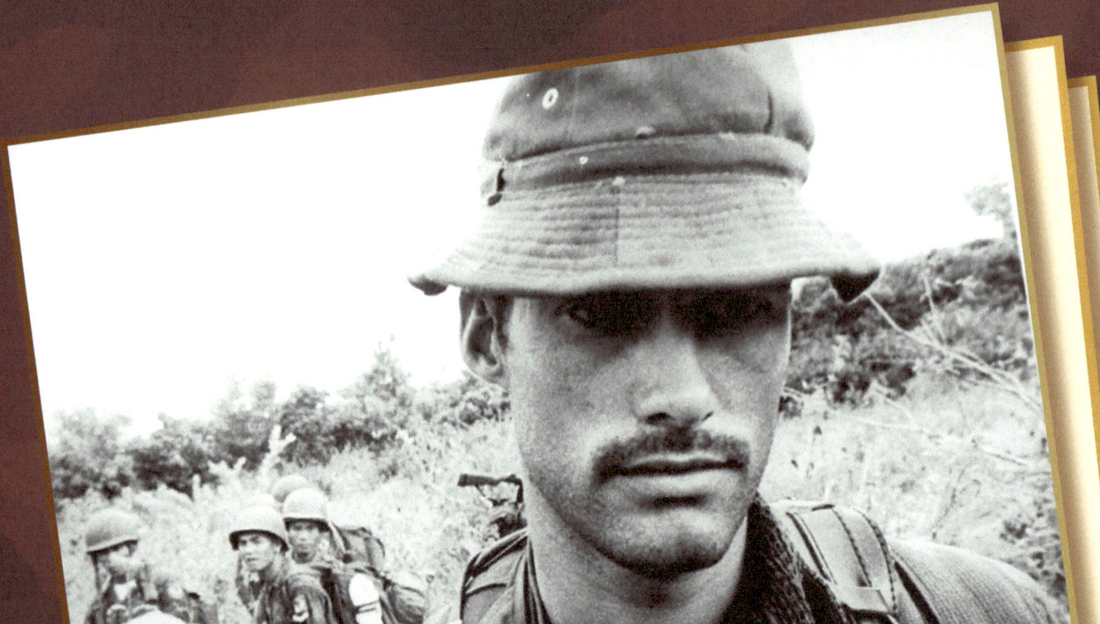

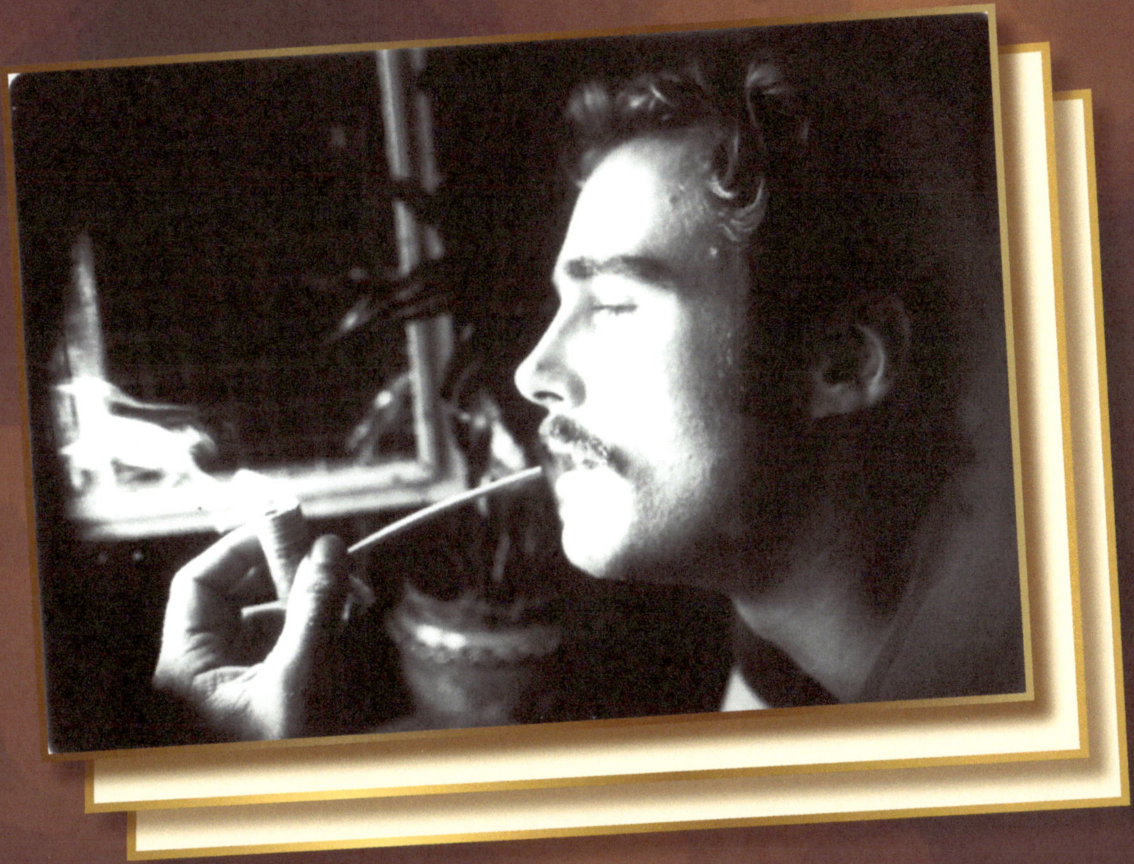

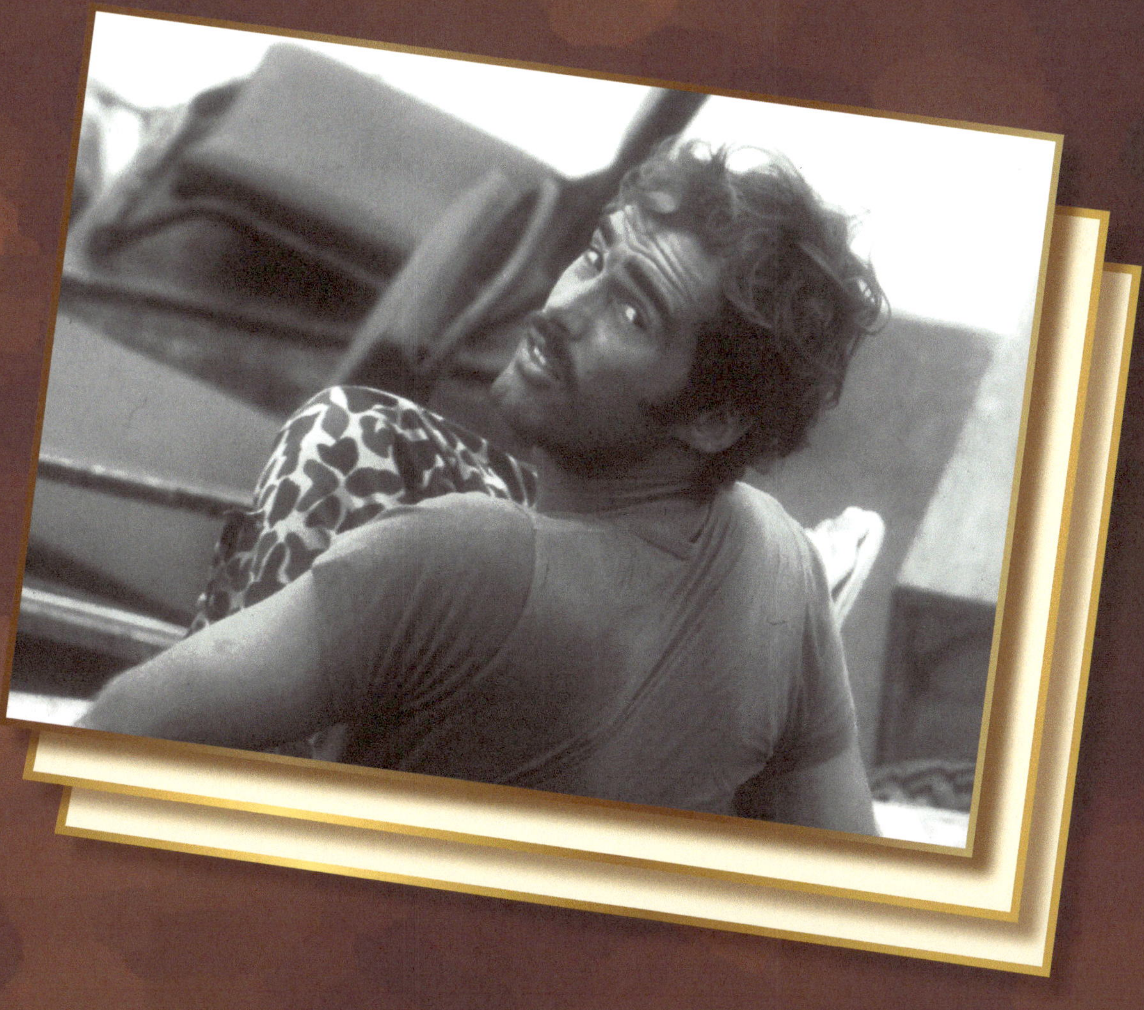

Vientiane
8 Mars '69
Dimanche

P.1 - before you read this get a map of S.E. Asia —

fait accompli: Four hundred kilometers to Luang Prabang the Royal Capital, repository of Buddha relic in a golden domed esophagus — up the Mekong to Pak Ou and a thousand Buddha statues in cliffs' cave, altogether memorable but hotel (only one) where I stayed depressingly occupied by shifts of Air America pilots, CIA etc as U.S. pushes another of her clandestine wars onto China's frontiers. U.S. everywhere in PX sport shirts arming, feeding, resettling, intriguing as any colonial power (and perhaps history has made the exercise of power inevitable for the powerful — the Russians broke in 1962 and packed up when Kennedy was pissed off — only the big powerful US left. DeGaulle was right) Trip beautiful from half way up starting at Vang Vieng. Sawtooth green mountains, pure clear streams, slightly chilly and nobody in sight except occasional Meo tribesman down from their opium growing in mountain top villages. Dressed in black with bright blue and Red brocaded hems, a kilo of family wealth in silver around wives' neck. Finally I find old friend pilot René, a legend, Senegalese, fighter pilot at Dien Bien Phu, flies 1935 DC3 with passengers and contraband, a completely charming rogue who flies me and moto (I bought a 100cc Yamaha scrambler) back here, opens cockpit door and with a wink gesticulates for me to come forward. In his chocolate fist a bottle of Dewars'. Gulp! go the passengers. But this is Laos and Damn! we clear the Luang Prabang mountains at nine thousand. Kharma working overtime again. Future project, get potful of visas, fly to Ban Houei Sai in west Laos on the Lao, Thai, Burmese border. Why? - Old fort Carnot is the center of the opium smuggling with expatriate Chinese Kuomingtan, Royal Army, C.I.A. and half a dozen ethnic minorities pushing and pulling for a piece of the action. Colorful adventure I hope. - Then with moto I scramble 100 kil. over and through mountains to Chiang Rai, head south to Bangkok, east to Pakse, south to Cambodian frontier and Khong Falls a natural wonder of the world, Phnom Penh favorite city south to Viet border and TRY to cross at Chau Doc (Chau Phu) Western SVN border city & whew! old rocket torn Saigon. My secret: be humble and a good Buddhist (but still a flesh eater)   we're driving and have Sony tape recorder playing Jimi Hendrix playing earphones — stop, groove, take pictures, speak Lao, Thai, French, Vietnamese but NEVER english ('someday I'll have to get a French passport) Any way theres sure to be a fuck up and maybe I'll get back eventually.

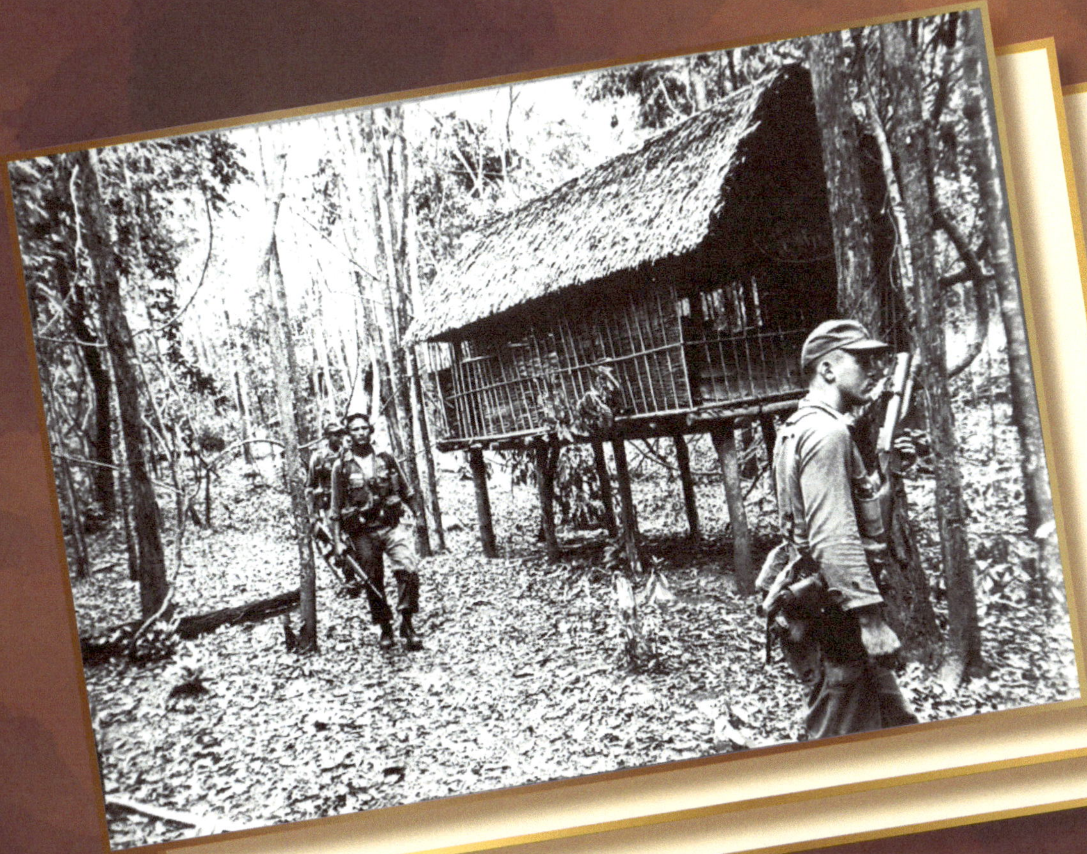

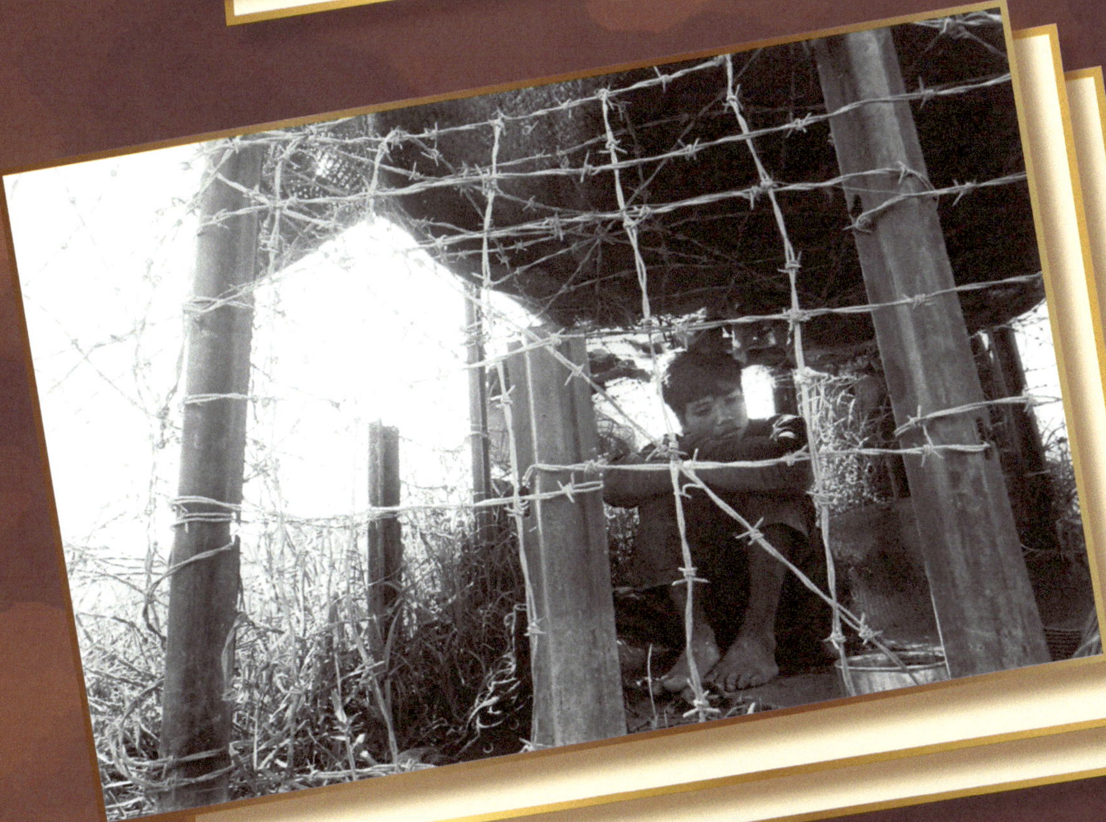

March 31/1969
monday

Now + lets see — where am I?

Ban Houei Sai I believe with future movements out of focus. Met friend of Crystals', Fred Cunningham, I've got boat went upriver to Burma. Many tribes here, scare you to death with their costumes but photographically neat — stayed with Yao's from China while Fred dug a well. Brought cycle with me here, staying at house but for 20₿ U Rent It. Nice here, peaceful maybe too much so. However in several years the refugees (26 ethnic tribes I believe) will have been McJuhanized and nobody has really tried to record their bag. As you can imagine this could take 6 months or a year — won't be here that long.

Reading the Bankok Post sent electro Pavlovian jolts thru these stoned bones when another big V.N. punchup with Cong fuckin nursed in the Pex at 5 PM on Sunday seemed imminent. But fuck, can't get hung on one thing.

This trip is weird.

Could you ask Page to sweat my return which will be next month on cycle thru Laos + Cambot etc. Would send a rent check but Stuff stolen sometimes see Fred River down to L.P. seems dubious water very low & boatmen getting shot up. Tempted to make trip north

to Vien Pou Kha but P.L. sneaking around in woods.

Actually this will take 2 weeks down but tho I'm tempted not to send it I realize something may delay.

Shit Jack, I may never leave Asia, tell John & Crystal that there is "possibility" for great work with tribes — every one will tell stories of the Past, ancestors, religion (saw a 200 yr old handwritten Dao Ching) they're going to go in a short time.

Burn a taper for the 'MC' of Wander, Best to all friends

S

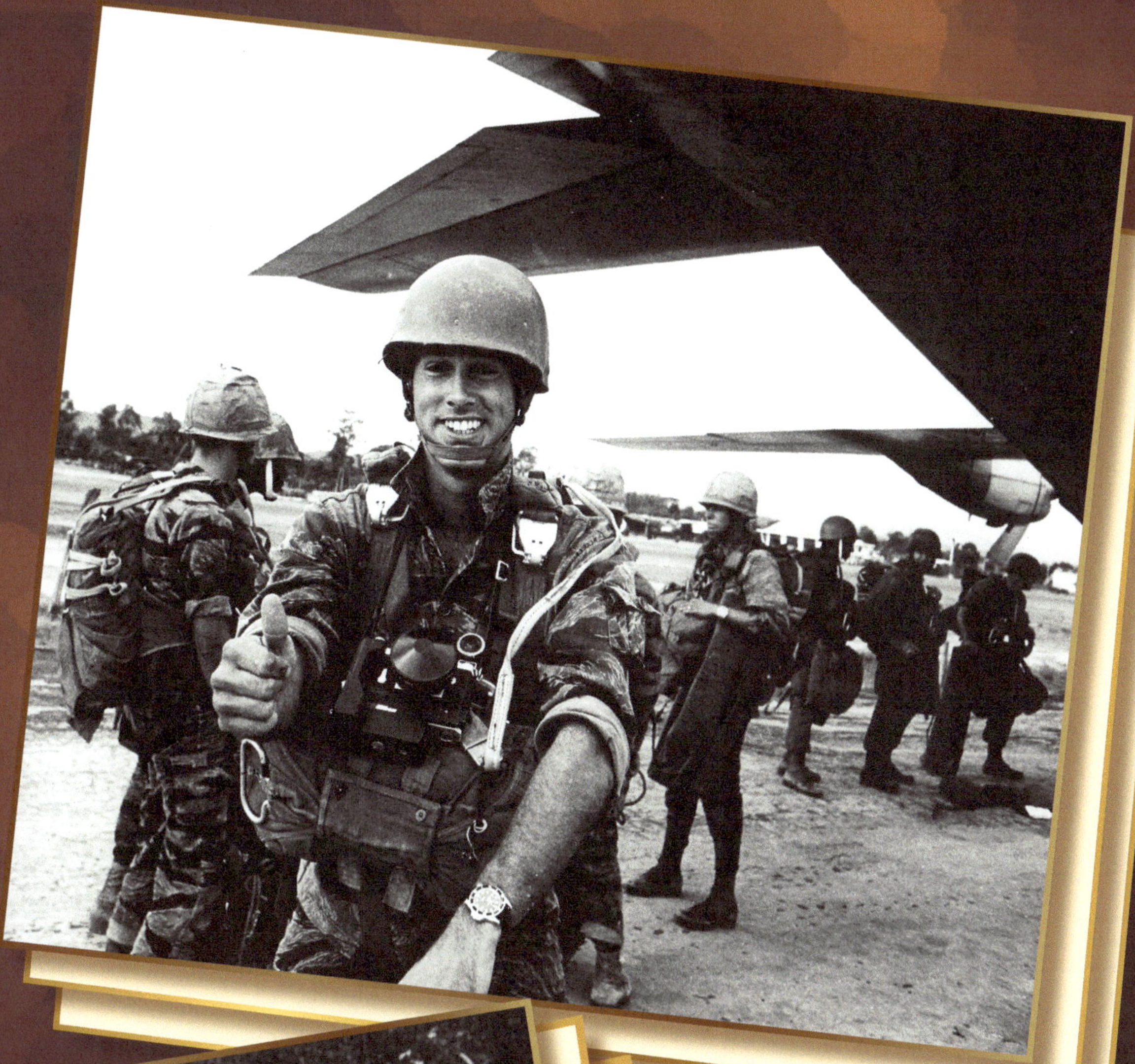

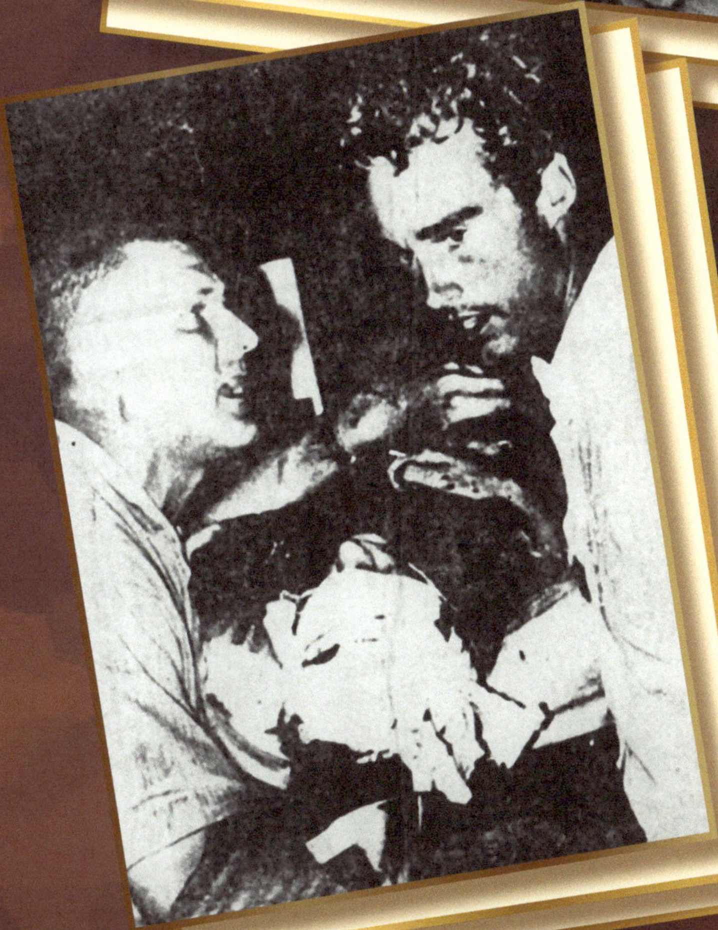

April 29 —
Saigon

So much has happened — how can I begin? Perhaps with Laos.

After leaving Vientiane I went north to Houei Sai on the Burmese border, traveled upriver and stayed with the Yao a nomadic Chinese people from Yunan now refugees. Very colorful, many photos — I was happy. After two weeks I returned to Vientiane hoping to travel south thru Laos to Cambodia. Thanks to a visa problem I did not leave when I had hoped. This proved fortunate. Five French were captured and shot in a town a short distance away thru which I would have gone. I waited for the "Pi-mi", the water festival and made plans to leave. On the eve of my departure I received a telegram from the embassy. Tim Page had been wounded, critically.

"Do you know how old I became so soon? I don't understand. I have seen so many dead and in some way I feel a part of them too.

Perhaps because I stayed here so long, I came here for adventure, returned to escape a technological bitter society.

Now. I am alone. All friends have left or been wounded like Phouc who had his eye shot out last month.
I was tempted to leave but to go where? I'd like to see the apartment and you but this isn't possible. The money I had will run out and even if there is some I must stop running and come to terms with my life. The freedom of my existential life, self-indulgent with no responsibilities is too much now. Too much freedom is not enough good work.

Saigon - 21 Oct.

I just returned from the demilitarized zone near north Vietnam where the U.S. Marines have been fighting a regular division People's Army force — it is a fierce war with torrential rains soaking everybody. 24 hrs. a day. I was glad to get away — too many correspondents anyway for me. I plan to make my first trip into the Delta, go out with the Vietnamese Rangers and go with the river boats that attack Viet Cong villages. I am supposed to be working for UPI on staff which is funny because a staff job is for life and very serious and I've never thought about any job for life but there are certain advantages in the deal and I told them that as conditions, I would go where I liked and photograph what I like and not be on any schedule — they said O.K.

Sout East Asia
is a funny drug — Opium as a habit — much worse than hard to break.!

I just returned from a month in Laos. I was trying to find the Nationalist Chinese in the North west but had little success. I stayed in Vientiane which is a fantastic place. Opium is legal California— the store must have a license to sell them, opium is sold on the counter in the morning paper. It costs 2 centimes for ... There are many hippies that hitchhike from west and there are several hippy restaurants "la tortuga" in ... but better have went south ... Frances Green, the son who is a ... character in ... we explored ... Khet north — about kilometers in ... trying to find or North V... these customs. It was quiet. We ... to some villages of the Meo and I ... some cloth that they I will send a ... back to you.

Also I will send you movie film. I'll send a telegram to you before I ship it. Then could you pick it up at Orly airport when the plane arrives and take it to:

Vitfer - 1 Rue Charles Marie Widor Paris 16
AUT 88-05

It is almost opposite the studio of Tony Kent. Ask them to develop and hold it there. The 50¢ is for development fee. — also did you ask the concierge to ... — also did you send my mail. I wrote you several letters didn't have a stamp one from the Sahn but dangerous place there P. Jesus that was a ... were so many jets that you couldn't hear ... rockets coming in the North Vietnamese

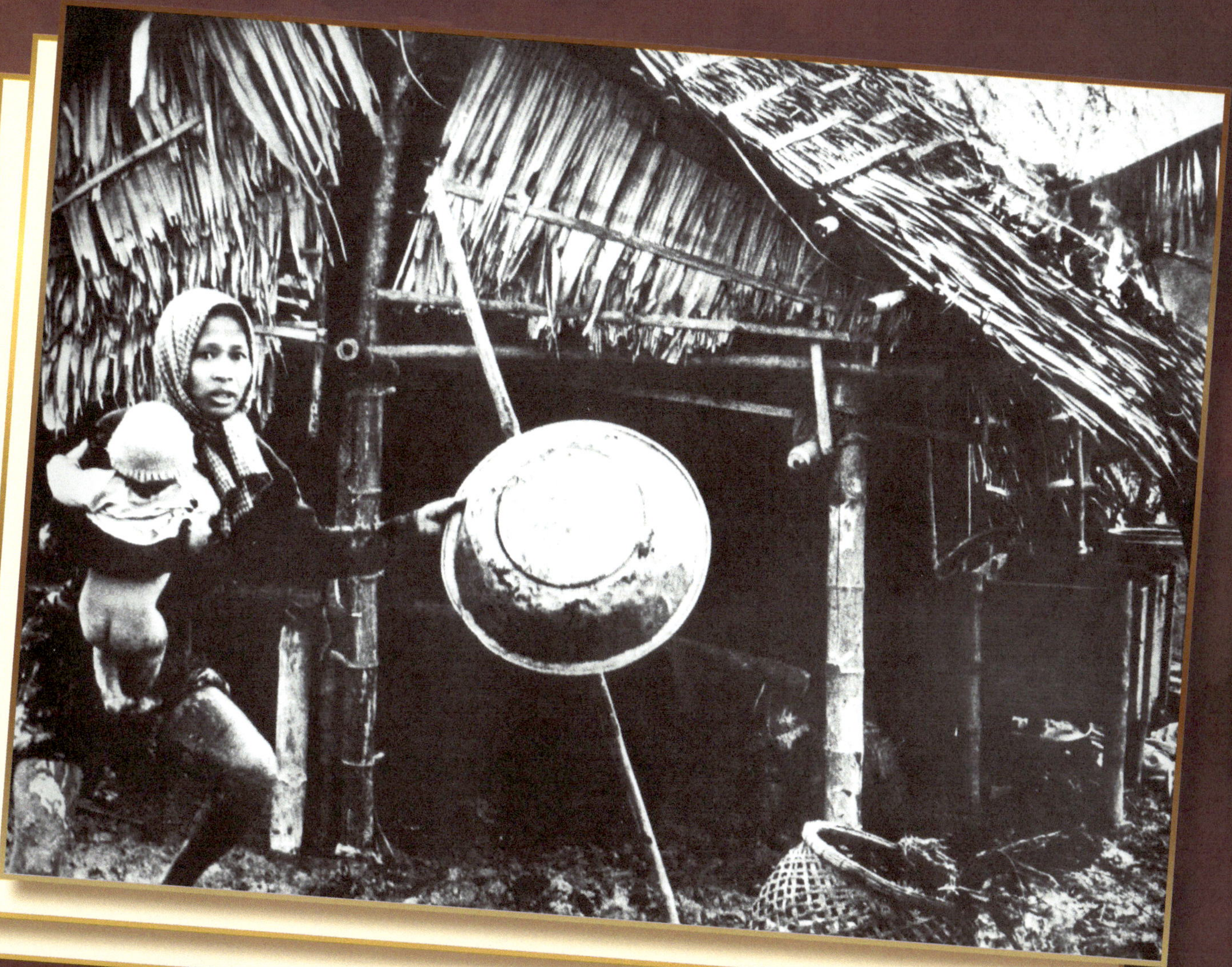

To describe my visit to Angor in which I spent riding a bicycle, listening to tape recorder, taking pictures etc. + drawing postcards, for the first time I feel 3/4 master of camera color photography. I sat in the ruins of the far out minor temples, alone, took photos of spiders, leaves, natives and the jungle.

What holds me up here is
1) caught a nasty parasitic disease which will be around a long time called hookworm, a dirty drag.
2) made plans to go out with Viet Cong during Christmas — maybe — it could be good
3) all in all I like Asia + have other projects but feel necessary to return to Paris + find out about things. Please write

---

July 13 1968

I'm in Saigon for a few days + then back to the DMZ + the Marines.

Your letter was a relief — Don't want to elaborate but people are trying to kill me with bombs + bullets so at least I want the film developed. —

all film in this package with the black tape is EKTACHROME MS — number 7256 the asa is 64. in the other package there was film with white tape. It's EKTACHROME EF number 7241 with asa 160 — All film is Daylight and not tungsten — if you have doubts show this to Vitter — if they don't understand them

Well I still feel good about here but the war is slowing down, fortunately there are friends, beaches, sail boats (which I really dig now!

I received a letter from Bob Leidy (name spelled wrong I bet) who asked about the war but to answer would take at least a day's work. — one has to describe not only military but social, agrarian and political ramifications also. A big task and one I don't have time for.

Its bloody hot out — yesterday 104 in the shade. Walking in the sun north of Hue on route 555 "The Street without Joy" in Bernard Fall's book of the same title is a white flat hot sandy 20 mile stretch. We had average 25 men per company lost to heat exhaustion — thats 100 men a battalion. Those kids are younger than me by ten years but after a while you get foxy and know where to move and how to move very important at 120 degree's summer heat. So I go to the beach in my spare time to get tanned, the theory being that tanned skin is more resistant to sun — an thats where I'm off to now

luv S

Singapore
March 10, 1970

Found a nice rooming house large, Victorian with large lawn. Next door lives guy & chick from Nepal with gibbon, down the hall a couple runaway American schoolgirls, a hairy rock band, a Chinese bargirl etc. Real Somerset Maugham 1970 style — no longer the boozy English pukka sahib but now the traveling hippy trip.

I didn't manage to get the land in Bali as my partner got a very serious case of malaria and had to be med-evaced. I shipped a couple crates back to Woodbridge — stone axes, bows & arrows from West Irian, paintings & wood sculptures etc from Bali & Java etc. — They will arrive around end of May.

I'm leaving for Saigon in a few days & will send you a nice package from there of some extraordinary batiks, modern & classic. You might want to put them on the wall. Anyway they are beautiful works of Art and I know they'll be safe with you.

I saw Laksmi at her convent in Djodjakarta — sister superior had orders not to let me in but she turned out to be right on and I got in. Laksmi was beautiful — I miss her very much. But plan to return Indonesia.

Singapore too fast — everybody on a rush businessman thing — these Chinese are just like Americans in that sense. However being free port I could replace the blue jeans & t-shirts & gadgets that somehow atrophy during a 7 month Indonesian stay.

One can get the latest records recorded onto tape cassette for a couple dollars, that would cost at least $10-$15 in the U.S. Also good books on Bali here. Weather OK. City relatively clean even.

Will write next from Saigon (maybe)

love SH

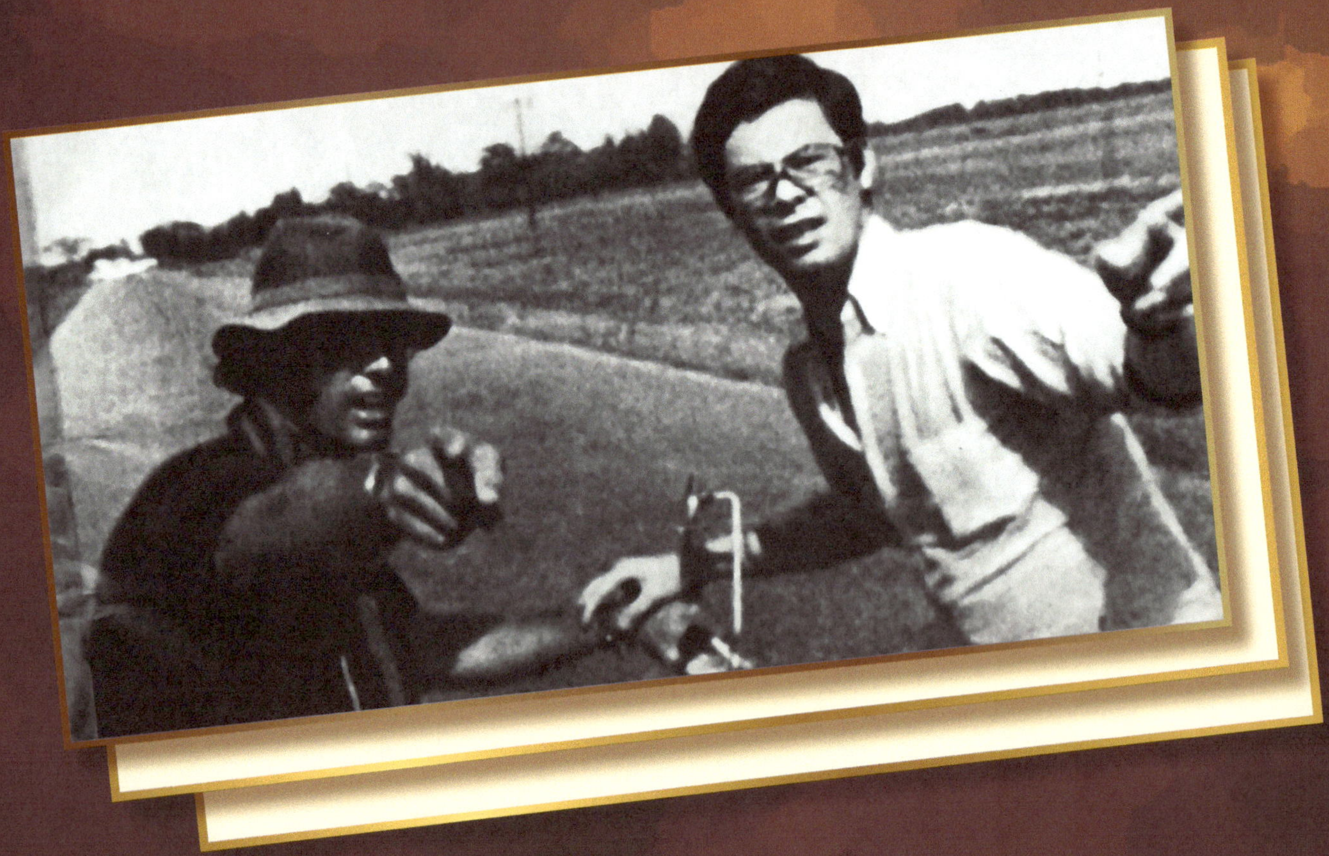

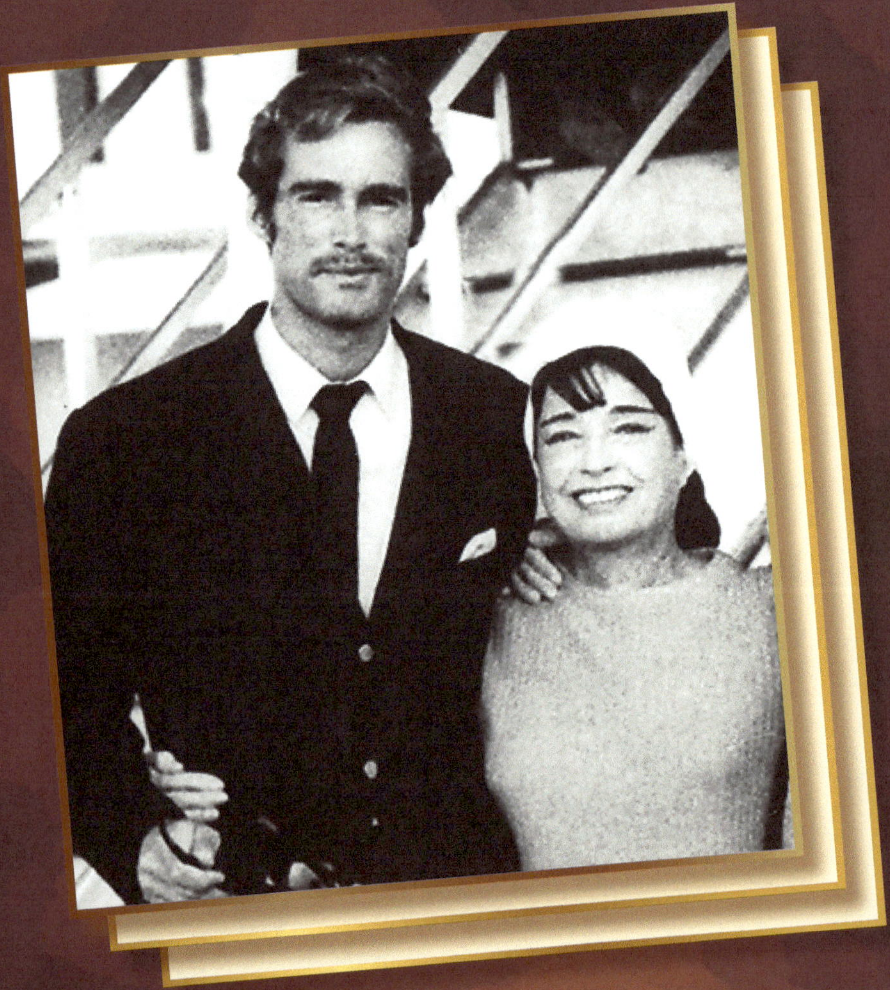

Chicago Tribune Oct-13-68

Sean Flynn, 27, son of the late actor, Erroll Flynn, has been wounded for a second time while working for a television network with U.S. troops in Vietnam. Flynn, who suffered chest wounds, lives in Paris. He previously was wounded in February, 1966.

The US Committee to Free Journalists Held in SE Asia (Walter Cronkite - Chairman) provided information depicted here - see page 2. Map drawn to scale 0 — 50 MILES — 50

THAILAND — **LAOS**

CAMBODIA

THAI-CAMBODIA BORDER — MEKONG RIVER — CAMBODIA-LAOS BORDER

4 - Numerous ARVN POWs released after cease-fire had heard journalists detained within a 50 mile radius of Kratie circled here as late as March 1973.

3 - NVA officer who defected saw 2 of 6 journalists held here May 30 1970.

6 - Cambodian national saw 10 Caucasians identified as Journalists here June 1972.

STUNG TRENG

5 - ARVN POW saw six Caucasians identified as Journalists here May 1972.

Source via U.S. State Dept. reports 2 Caucasian and 7 Asian Journalists here 1973.

ROUTE 13 — KRATIE — SNUOL — VIETNAM-CAMBODIA BORDER

KOMPONG CHAM — CHUP — MIMOT — ROUTE 7 — LOC NINH

PHNOM PENH

SOUTH VIETNAM

2 - Five Journalists captured here - May 31, 1970

ROUTE 3 — SVAY RIENG — ROUTE 1 — ROUTE 22 — TAY NINH

1 - Ten of 18 still missing journalists captured here April 1970.

MEKONG — VIETNAM-CAMBODIA BORDER

SAIGON

APRIL 2, 1970   Bankok

Have traveled fast & high since last letter (sent you salak fruit tree seeds in box from Singapore) - I returned 10 days ago to Saigon - saw old friend Jack Laurence of CBS who asked me to go with him for two months to make documentary - we spent few days near Cambodian border but things were popping there & I got Time (good old Time) to send me to Phom Penh - I'm going in 15 minutes so just have enough time to get fast — Had to stop here first for visa - looks like near civil war there since Sihanouk's demise (too bad - I dug his neutrality - he leaked off the U.S. & Russia because he didn't "play" the diplomatic game by their rules - he was a hip ruler like Canada's Trudeau or even Sukarno in his own way - nationalist first, & above all else. Looks like I'll be busy here in Indochina for awhile yet with Laos & Cambodia hot.

Before I forget - THANK YOU Madre mia for the book on West Irian you sent, also the 3 monkey ward shirts and the two grand. When things cool I'll probably go back to Bali - don't worry - its a good investment for your HEART not to be forgotten among the other property you mentioned possibly selling — I would suggest you examine ways to get $ out of the U.S. to say, Switzerland. I hesitate to suggest business suggestions for it's your bread but you can always count on me for whatever when you want impartial (as far as possible) advice. Just this idea — that all things here in this world are God's toys - you, me, bread, Cambodia etc. Make peace with them & your heart is still — do you know how to do it?

Watch the bugs, plants, sunsets, rains, the change of wind, the sea, clouds & watch them and relax in peace — there is a place for us all.

must go —

love
S

Epilogue

Errol Flynn

Despite the fact that my father had always been clear about his wish to be buried under an oak tree on his beloved estate in Jamaica, his estranged widow, Pat Wymore, who, apparently had felt humiliated by my father because he had taken a much younger girlfriend for the last two years of his life, had him interred in an unmarked plot in Forest Lawn Memorial Park of Glendale, California. In 1979, twenty years after his death (over riding the widow's instructions), my sister Deirdre and I had a bronze plaque placed on the gravesite, which lies next to that of Ida Lupino's mother. It reads "In Memory of Our Father, from his Loving Children," and today fans still gather there each year on June 20th to commemorate his birth. He never knew how much pleasure and happiness he brought to his fans around the world.

Mulholland Farm

Upon the Baron's death, his still-single first wife was awarded the Farm for back alimony; soon after, she remarried, this time to the wealthy inventor of Eskimo pies. From her the Farm passed through a succession of owners, including singer and onetime teen idol Rick Nelson, who bought it in 1981 and owned it at the time of his death in an airplane crash four years later. The subsequent owner bought the Farm for $1 million, demolished the buildings on it and, in 1988, sold the land for development at a substantial profit.

Errol Flynn Estates (in Jamaica)

His final will in which, so he had told my mother several times, he had left nothing to his several wives but everything to the children- mysteriously disappeared, and my father's widow, P. Wymore, with the assistance of my father's attorney, Justin Goldenbach, produced a will which—left everything to her.

My mother, of course, set out to contest that will, optimistic about the outcome because she knew someone, the wife of another well-known actor and a friend to my father, who had witnessed the signing of the missing will and could verify its provisions.

When the case got to court, however, my mother's witness suddenly declined to testify—in this paranoid era of the Hollywood blacklists and smear campaigns, she was afraid that her association with my father would adversely affect her husbands career.

In the end, Wymore took everything, including ownership of Jamaica. For his part, the attorney was awarded ownership of my father's beloved sailboat, The Zaca.

Errol Flynn's declared last will and testament of April 27, 1954, was in probate for fourteen years. Finally, under the terms of that will, legal title of the Errol Flynn properties in Jamaica, like the rest of his estate, passed to his estranged widow.

The Zaca
During the 14-year probate period, my father's sailing ship lay untended — and uncared for — at anchor.

The Zaca was then sold to a well-to-do European fan of my father's who undertook the massive restoration the ship needed. Today the Zaca is a popular tourist attraction in Villefrance, on the Mediterranean near the city of St. Tropez.

Sean
After trying his hand at several careers, my brother found great meaning as a photojournalist covering the war in Vietnam for more than six years. When Nixon ordered the secret bombing of Cambodia, Sean, along with several of his fellow photojournalists, crossed the border to obtain evidence of the bombing campaign for the world to see. He was subsequently captured by the Khmer Rouge and never seen alive again. The search to solve the mystery of his fate continues.

Deirdre
Always an outstanding athlete, my sister enjoyed success as a stuntwoman in action films, doubling for such stars as Michael Douglas. Her specialties included a variety of stunts involving horses, motorcycles and fast cars. Deirdre is currently alive and well and living in Los Angeles.

Arnella
I shared more of my life with her than with anyone else, having lived together in both London and New York, and having spent our holidays together in Jamaica for some 20 years before her tragic death in 1998. I never heard her say an unkind word about anyone, but I'm afraid she was too fragile for life as a Flynn. There isn't a day that goes by that I don't miss my best friend and sister.

Luke and Sean (Rio)
The next generation of Flynns, the two grandsons; Luke and Sean , are healthy and handsome. At the age of thirty and having inherited his grandfather's looks, physique and charm, Luke, Arnella's son, worked as a model in New York and Miami since the age of six. Currently, his acting career is beginning to take off and he is also researching a career in writing. When he first tried his hand in Hollywood, Luke stayed with my family for a year, during which time he became like a big brother to my son Sean (Rio).

Sean, who is sixteen and clearly having inherited his grandfather's talent for entertaining — not to mention a certain fearlessness in the face of new challenges — Sean has been an actor in feature films and on television since the age of six. At this time he is the male lead on 'ZOEY 101" a series for Nickelodeon, going into its third season. He is a guitar player and a student.

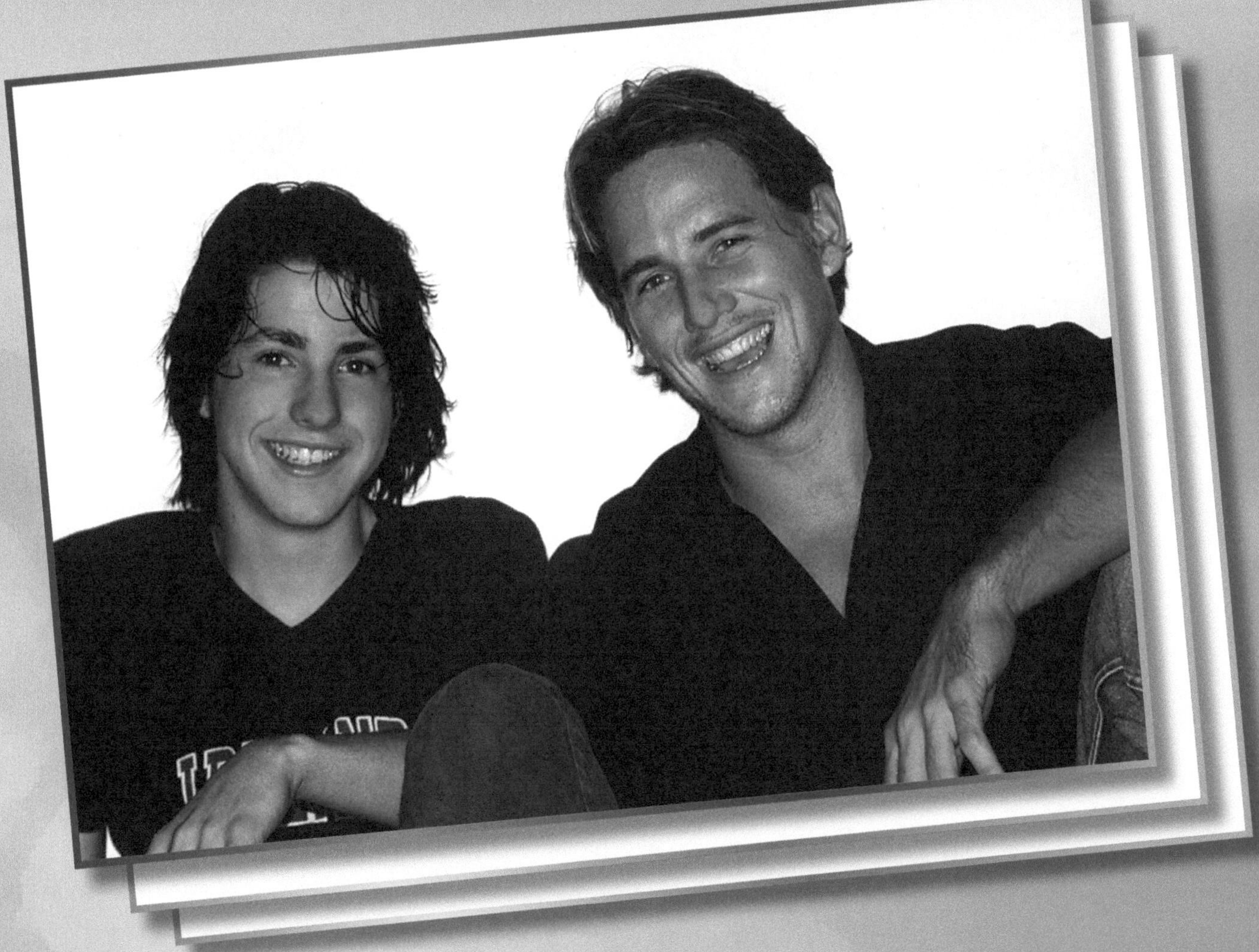